Feeling Good About Me

By

Kenneth Morrison

and

Marcia Thompson

Focus-Feeling Sessions for Self-Image Development

for Elementary School Facilitators

Educational Media Corporation®
P.O. Box 21311
Minneapolis, Minnesota 55421

Library of Congress Catalog Card No. 79-55664

ISBN 0-932796-05-2 Soft cover

Manufactured in the United States of America.

Production editor—

Don L. Sorenson

Graphic design—

Earl Sorenson

Illustrations—

Irv Sorenson

Printing (Last Digit)

10 9 8 7 6 5

Foreword

One of the most significant contributions to education in the past decade has been the introduction of "feelings" into the school curriculum. For too many years, the emotional aspect of learning was neglected in favor of an almost exclusive focus on traditional content and cognitive structures. The "self: as learner was too often viewed as peripheral to intellectual achievement. Now, most educators recognize that feelings are an inseparable part of any learning situation and that positive feelings about self and others are essential to effective learning.

Teachers, counselors, parents, and peers play an important part in building childrens' self-concepts. With the help of selected educational experiences, such as the eighteen structured sessions outlined in *Feeling Good About Me*, they can provide a stimulating climate where young people are supported and encouraged to explore and learn more about themselves and the world around them.

Ken Morrison and Marcia Thompson present a set of prepared activities that facilitators of learning—teachers and students—can use to help children develop more positive and realistic self-images. As we have all come to realize, feeling good about one's self is an inextricable part of enjoying life and learning.

Robert D. Myrick, Ph.D.
Counselor Education
University of Florida
Gainesville, Florida

DEDICATION

This book is dedicated
to
Mary Kay and Mitch
Morrison
and
Kevin and Stacey
Thompson

Table of Contents

Preface

"The most precious gift we give a child is a positive and realistic self-image."

H. Ginolt

It is our belief that the most disadvantaged children in society today are those children suffering from a lack of positive self-image—those children who in one way or another have learned not to feel good about themselves. Too often, due to a number of variables, many pre school children already have learned not to feel good about themselves.

While evidence of lack of positive self-image is available at an early age, it is usually not until children enter school that the associated problems begin to surface. As some children move from family life to the more formal and structured environment of the school, the ramifications of this lack of positive self-image are most readily seen. The resulting behaviors are most frequently demonstrated in the following ways: behavior problems, lack of general academic achievement, unexcused absences and negative overall attitudes about school.

The combination of a new environment, multi-peer interactions and the entrance of a new significant adult teacher in their lives seems to be too much for children without sufficient positive self-images to handle. As if these variables were not enough, these children also are faced with the problem of achievement.

Therefore, some children seem to find themselves in a cyclic trap. The lack of positive self-image causes difficulties in school and the school difficulties cause further lack of positive self-image.

Other children, even those with reasonably positive self-images, often become bewildered by their worlds and struggle with their feelings about self. This struggle can lead to self-image problems, if left unattended.

We concur with Purkey (1970) that it is a personal tragedy and social waste when children spend year after year experiencing defeat and failure in the schools. The causes of failure and the effects of the failing experience are complex, but a continuous and central factor in both cause and effect is the way students view themselves and their abilities.

We believe, as Nelson (1972) believes, that the self emerges as a consequence of learning experiences with other human beings and the introspection of their values and attitudes. We also believe, as Weisse, Dickmann and Morrison (1976) believe, that children's perceptions are their realities as they stress to actualize, to maintain and to enhance self.

Further, we agree with Dobson and Dobson (1976) when they suggest that self-image growth experiences for children should focus on children's perceptions and feelings relative to life events. Then they may grow toward a position of ordering and controlling their environment, as opposed to merely reacting to it.

Therefore, the thrust of our work is to assist children in acceptance of personal feelings and the development of positive feelings about self. It is our contention that children can develop positive self-images. If given the opportunity, children will move toward positive self-growth.

REFERENCES

Dobson, R. & Dobson, J. *Humanness in Schools: A Neglected Force*. Dubuque, IA: Kendall/Hunt Publishing Company, 1976.

Nelson, R. C. *Guidance and Counseling in the Elementary School.* New York, NY: Holt, Rinehart and Winston, 1972.

Purkey, W. W. *Self-Concept and School Achievement*. Englewood Cliffs, NJ: Prentice-Hall, 1970.

Weisse, E. B., Dickmann, L. W. & Morrison, K. *The Symmetrical Teacher*. Dubuque, IA: Kendall/Hunt Publishing Company, 1976.

Introduction

PURPOSE, FORMAT AND GOALS

The purpose of this book is to aid children in their school experience. It is our contention that children will learn the basics of education more readily if, in the process, children also learn to share and accept feelings and thereby come to feel better about themselves.

The format of this program is a series of eighteen structured focus-feeling sessions for positive self-image building. Each session is a self-contained unit, so the sessions may be used separately or as a developmental sequence.

The primary goals of this book are to help children:

1. Identify and accept personal feelings.
2. Develop positive feelings about self.
3. Accept responsibility for feelings and actions.
4. Develop positive self-images.

Before introducing you to the key elements featured in each of the eighteen sessions, we would first like to make some general observations about the importance of having an accepting atmosphere and a supportive environment. We suggest that the leaders function as facilitators in order to best aid children in becoming more aware and responsive to their own feelings.

ATMOSPHERE

We have found that this program and the activities involved seem to work best in an accepting atmosphere. Such an atmosphere takes time to develop and cannot be forced. Each experience, personal and group, is unique and should be allowed the freedom to be one of a kind.

The activities are used to guide and not to control the experience. A sudden turn of events or sharing within the needs of those involved should be allowed and even cultivated. Since no program can predict exact needs, we believe this program can be used to create an atmosphere to nurture opportunities for exploration and awareness.

Children should be allowed to develop and grow at their own speed within this program and this, in itself, helps create an atmosphere where there is freedom and safety. The safety to share or not to share—the safety to grow or not to grow—will occur when trust is openly communicated to all involved.

This trust will develop with time, experience and risk taking. The more children can trust each other to laugh, to cry, to hurt, to be angry, to be afraid and to be loving together, the more they will feel safe and free to be and to become. Such experiences will help individuals trust themselves in a positive way and approach their world in the same manner.

ENVIRONMENT

Trust and acceptance may be partially communicated by the choice of the physical setting. Our experiences suggest that a safe and relaxed setting is most helpful for personal learning. If available, we have often chosen a special room (or space in the room) where interruptions can be avoided. At times we have found soft rugs or pillows to be an asset. Also, the addition of personal items such as toys, plants, pictures, blankets and books can help create a feeling of belonging. This sharing can help develop not only self awareness, but respect and responsibility for others.

The use of soft music in the background can be explored as a possible addition to creating a feeling of safety and warmth. Dim lighting will, when appropriate, also make sharing feel much safer than in bright light. The size of the area chosen should be one where students feel safe but not constricted. A large area may tend to make students feel small and somewhat lost, where a crowded area might not allow for necessary physical and emotional freedom.

Such an area that can provide both safety and freedom may need to be created by the use of tables, chairs, curtains, dividers and other moveable objects. The physical moving of equipment in preparation for a special time together can provide a pre-experience focus and become a vital part of sharing, cooperating and assuming responsibility.

If a separate and set environment is available, pre-experience focus activities might be used. It is important, however, to use three to four different activities over the period that the program continues so that there is a sense of continuity and reliability. Such activities can be rotated on a daily, weekly or unit basis.

Pre-focus Activities

The following are suggestions to help set the stage for focus-feeling sessions:

1. Wear or carry a special, significant and personal item, which can change according to individual needs (i.e. toys, jewelry, clothing, books).
2. Create a special badge or sign with a group or personal message (i.e. I CARE, I HOPE, I SHARE, I TRY, I CAN).
3. Listen to and/or sing with the song *Free to Be* by Marlo Thomas. Other songs on the album by the same name may also be used.
4. Sing a favorite song or play a favorite game.
5. Let the children and facilitator freely roam an area for two or three minutes, each choosing a path to the set environment. Persons can choose positive, private thoughts to take with them on the walk.
6. Provide three to four minutes of physical exercise followed by three to four minutes of resting.

Physically moving to a special and specific environment, where experiences and time have established a place to hide, to laugh, to cry and to feel safe, is invaluable. Once established, such an environment will provide the support unit necessary for individuals to risk and grow outside of it. This special area can also become a place that individuals or groups can use to deal with special feelings or concerns.

FACILITATOR

The term "facilitator" is used throughout the program since it best represents the attitude desired for someone in the position of leadership. Facilitators are persons who provide opportunities for growth and change—*and nothing more.*

We suggest that facilitators of this program should:

1. Be willing to share openly and honestly with others.
2. Desire personal growth for self and others.
3. Accept children as they are.
4. Listen reflectively and believe in each child's desire and ability to seek, see and solve one's own problems.
5. Be willing to support individuals when they are ready to change and grow.
6. See success in self and others and be willing to share them.
7. Participate in activities as well as facilitate them.

Facilitators are both leaders and participants, with the role of participant being foremost. Facilitators can not expect any more involvement from the children than they are willing to give themselves. This open and honest sharing by facilitators can and will develop as the program progresses. It is, however, a vital role and may be the special ingredient that makes the program successful or unsuccessful.

Persons unsure of their ability to share in such a manner might work with a co-facilitator, or try many of the program's activities with a small group of friends as a personal warm-up before beginning.

Such a warm-up experience is not limited to just those facilitators with concerns, but it is excellent preparation for all facilitators. Some additional warm-up activities might include:

1. Write yourself a letter about hopes, dreams and fears. Give it to a friend and perhaps receive a reply.
2. Make a clay shape or a drawing of yourself as a facilitator. Share it with a friend and ask for honest feedback.
3. Do or say something you have been thinking about for some time.
4. Identify a set number of feelings each day and share them with someone.
5. Sit in one of the children's desks and talk as if you were that child.
6. Ask someone for help and support in an area of concern.
7. Reach out to an outsider and reflect on your feelings about the experience.
8. Share a personal experience with your students.

This program ***should not*** be facilitated by everyone. However, persons need not fear failure if they do not feel comfortable with such a program. We all communicate differently. The facilitation of this program is more likely to be successful if the concept of acceptance is emphasized.

The development of a positive self-image involves the acceptance of *all* feelings. Acceptance does not mean that the facilitator agrees with or condones all feelings, but rather it means that the feelings are heard in a non-judgmental manner.

When one can accept *all* of one's feelings and can assume responsibility to self and others within the framework of being fully human, then positive self-image development will more likely occur.

CHILDREN

This program is written for children—children who today are often finding themselves suffocating in a world of pent-up emotions and feelings.

Today's young people are faced with ever growing rules on one side and with an expanding freedom on the other. These conditions set children up for confusion as to how to think, act or feel. Too often children are put in an ever closing box of rules (i.e. school, parents, society, peers) while the door is left open to explore the unknown (i.e. drugs, alcohol, running away, vandalism).

Many children are not allowed by their environments to experience the uniqueness of being children. The right to be children full of life and to have a safe place to grow within limits is an endangered environment for our young people.

Children are limited in many ways, but the most devastating is that of limiting the gift of being human. There is no greater joy than to feel alive—alive with happiness, hurt, anger, sorrow, fear and love. This program offers one way of releasing or rekindling the best alternative—the gift of life. It offers the opportunity of discovering the uniqueness of self and the specialness of others.

With time and the experiences presented in this program, we believe that children can once again reclaim the gift and joy of life. Life can become the greatest adventure if we allow ourself to *feel*, to *be* and to *become.*

When children are given freedom to grow at their own pace in a safe and accepting environment, their true potential will be released. Some children make giant strides, others may only seem to take small steps—and some may seem not to change at all. But the success of this program is difficult to measure since sometimes a new thought, idea for feeling, takes longer than these eighteen sessions to show itself in action.

Therefore, these structured focus-feeling sessions should be only the first step in freeing feelings, accepting responsibility and positively experiencing life. The new positive self-image that this program can help create must continue to be nurtured.

Key Elements in the Program

The eighteen structured sessions are divided into six groups of three sessions each. The six groups focus on Happy, Angry, Sad, Unkind, Fear and Good feelings.

Each unit of three sessions contains an introduction to the unit and information for preparing the materials to be used in the three sessions to follow.

Each session contains the following elements:

1. RATIONALE:

The rationale is a statement used to motivate student interest and insight in that particular session.

2. GOALS:

The goals aid in planning and providing direction for the activities in each session. Also, the goals articulate the relationships among the various learning experiences within a session and among all the sessions.

3. MATERIALS:

The materials for each session are listed in the preparation section for each unit and at the beginning of each individual session. These materials are designed to be simple and inexpensive, but effective for use with children.

4. THOUGHT CATCHERS:

Thought Catchers are Mother Goose rhymes that can be used at the beginning of each session. The use of these rhymes provides an initial focusing on the feelings presented and as a warm-up for the process activities that follow.

5. PROCESS ACTIVITIES:

Process Activities provide the impetus for personal and interpersonal communications which are key elements in positive self-image development. It is important that the facilitator pay particular attention to these activities since they are closely related to the success of the program.

A. Discussion Starters:

A list of questions is provided for each session to break the ice and to aid group discussion.

B. Sharing Time:

This is unstructured time in the program; it should be used progressively more as the sessions develop. This time will also be beneficial in gauging the development of trust. As trust develops and grows, the use of *Sharing Time* will provide some of the most vital and important opportunities for self-expression and acceptance.

C. Reinforcement Activities:

These experiences provide the real testing ground of the basic ideas of self-responsibility. The self-responsibility experiences should begin at low-risk levels and build in group goals and progress to higher risk levels and individually set goals.

Remember, rewards and positive encouragement are very important to this type of learning activity—the idea is to move toward a self-motivated goal and self-reinforcement (an individual reward system).

Reinforcement Activities are introduced in the first session of each unit of three and played in the second and third sessions. These responsibility activities provide the opportunity for a powerful carry-over of new ideas and behavior into the children's world. The games are highly recommended as a meaningful method of reinforcement. Rewards for the completion of each game are also important tools of reinforcement.

D. Suggested Rewards:

Rewards are earned by children through the completion of the *Reinforcement Activities. Rewards* can be chosen by children as a group, as individuals or by the facilitator. Some lessons have *Suggested Rewards* which have been chosen because they supplement and reinforce the feelings or ideas being explored in those sessions.

However, the choice of *Rewards* and the methods of choosing them are optional. *Rewards* should be produced at the completion of the *Reinforcement Activities* or the power of the activities will be greatly diminished.

E. Reinforcement Stickers:

These stickers are another method of carrying ideas from the structured sessions into the children's world. The *Reinforcement Stickers* remind the children of the responsibility they have in their physical, social and emotional lives. The stickers are also a reward for finishing a series of sessions.

Materials: *Reinforcement Stickers* can be made from a variety of materials all the way from paper to cloth. The material recommended is IRON ON PATCHES which can be permanently pressed onto shirts, pants, books and so forth. The stickers can be made by the facilitator or by the children. An indelible ink pen is needed to insure the permanence of the message on the patches.

Reinforcement Sticker Examples

Happy Sticker
Lesson 3

Angry Sticker
Lesson 6

Sad Sticker
Lesson 9

Unkind Sticker
Lesson 12

Fear Sticker
Lesson 15

Good Sticker
Lesson 18

6. CURRICULAR-RELATED ACTIVITIES:

The feelings dealt with in the *Thought Catchers* are also the focus for a number of creative activities presented to help children get directly involved in the learning experience. These activities are related to specific subject matter area of the curriculum such as: art, drama, gym (physical education) and a language arts activity which is called "forming."

A. Art:

The art activity is designed as an extension of the main thrust of that particular session, but with an emphasis on the creative use of art material. This additional activity gives the child the opportunity to express feelings using a different media which can often produce new insights about self and others. All the art activities are based on the theme found in that session's *Thought Catcher*.

B. Drama:

Drama provides an expansive and creative way of discovering the human experience for both actor and audience. The drama activities allow the child the safety to act out and experience a variety of feelings and thoughts. Hiding inside a role, which is found in that session's *Thought Catcher*, the child is free to explore areas that might be too risky in the real world. Each drama activity is short enough to allow a number of students the opportunity to participate.

C. Gym (Physical Education):

The gym activity is another opportunity to explore further the basic feeling of that particular session. Once again, the *Thought Catcher* is used as the basic idea out of which comes the physical activity. These gym activities provide the child with a free and open opportunity to further explore relationships, responsibility and self-awareness.

D. Forming (Language Arts):

Forming is the term used to describe the experience of taking ideas and feelings and putting them in some written form. These activities are provided as another outreach opportunity for exploring personal feelings and thoughts. Self-expression in written form allows children one more means of discovering who they are and hope to be.

7. PRETENDING TIME:

Pretending Time is one more method of exploring, discovering and releasing the potential self. *Pretending Time* provides structured exercises that free children to ponder, pretend and expand personal hopes, dreams and wishes. It also reminds children that the skill of pretending is an important and acceptable means of practicing and preparing for life.

Pretending Time is always very personal and needs to be treated with great respect. The facilitator must remember that sharing is never expected, only *allowed*. Experience, trust and time will expand the scope and sharing of *Pretending Time.* It may take three to four attempts before some children can begin to free their imaginations.

Each *Pretending Time* begins with a three to four minute *Ready-Set-Go* and always ends with a two or three minute *Stop-Look-Listen* followed by *Reflections*. The beginning, ending and review phases, plus the pretending itself, should be done in a quiet, relaxed and uninterrupted environment. *Pretending Time* is planned to take 15-20 minutes and this amount of time should be available before the process is started.

Pretending Time is a process with a beginning, a middle, an end and a follow-up. It is not something that one jumps into or out of in a brief time. The time and effort to do *Pretending Time* will prove itself in value and worth as the program expands.

The facilitator of *Pretending Time* helps set a safe, comfortable and caring environment by using a relaxed body position and a soft and quiet voice tone. The facilitator's awareness of the importance of both verbal and non-verbal clues will allow *Pretending Time* to be an adventure and a positive learning experience.

A. Ready-Set-Go:

Children find a relaxed position on the floor or in chairs and are asked to close their eyes. (Positions with feet propped up or with the body in odd positions are not conducive for *Pretending Time.*) Specific suggestions for *Ready-Set-Go* are given in each session.

This phase is aimed at relaxing both body and mind, but it is also used to release the child from thoughts about previous experiences and to begin centering or focusing on a new area.

B. Pretending:

The . . . always means a pause in time so the pretending can take place. The pause in time will vary from 1/2 to 2 minutes and depends on facilitator and group needs at that particular time.

Pretending Time is *not* to be interrupted as interruptions can cause the flow to be broken and the mood of the experience difficult to regain.

C. Stop-Look-Listen:

At the end of *Pretending*, the facilitator asks the children to slowly stop pretending and to be prepared to think about what has been learned.

D. Reflections:

Reflections provide the time to discuss what was learned by those who desire to do so. Since all the *Pretendings* are very personal experiences and also very new experiences to most young people, the sharing is not required, only made available. It is suggested that the facilitator experience *Pretending Time* beforehand to be able to share that experience and model an open mood for the rest of the group, especially for the first two or three *Pretending Times.* Also, sharing small parts of the *Pretending* instead of the whole thing may be most helpful and provide solid ground for future sharing.

The interpretation or meaning of *Pretending Time* is left entirely to each person experiencing it. *Reflections* is only a sharing phase and not one of reactions. If interpretations do occur, then sharing will dwindle and the learning about self and others will be lost.

8. FABLES:

The fable selected for each session emphasizes the particular focus feeling for the session and allows children to become more involved through the medium of the story.

9. SUPPLEMENTAL ACTIVITIES:

These activities are minor elements of the program. However, we have found them to be very helpful considering the small amount of time needed for each activity.

Sense Stretchers—

Sense Stretchers provide experiences that not only expand the area of feelings, but also expand the area of sensory awareness. The more aware we become to the smells, sounds, sights, and tastes in our world, the more alive we will become as people and the less fearful we will be of the unknown.

Sense Stretchers can be one or more of the activities suggested for each session. The facilitator can choose to use whichever activities best fit the group of children, the available material and the time allotted.

Examples

1. Eyes (seeing):

Items are brought in that visually elicit the particular focus feeling. An example of this would be a photo or object from or about an event or experience that was happy, sad and so forth.

2. Ears (hearing):

Children are asked to quickly and ramdomly share words or phrases that bring forth that session's focus feeling. Examples might be: "I Like You"—"Bad Boy"—"Run Quick"— "Dummy"—"Stupid"—"Princess."

3. Nose (smelling):

Visits to a bakery, florist, bank, grocery store, newspaper office or factory give small groups opportunities to identify and list various smells. The group with the longest list could be called "super smellers" and get badges made in the shape of a nose.

4. Tongue (tasting):

The children can experience a new ethnic meal. A trip to a restaurant or a home, or a meal prepared by the children, can make this activity long-remembered.

10. P. S. (POST SCRIPT) ACTIVITIES—

P. S. (Post Script) Activities can be used by the facilitator to creatively fill in those short waiting periods before lunch, recess, assemblies and dismissal times.

Examples

1. Poem Pushers:

Poem Pushers are nothing more than favorite poems read or recited in such a way as to express one of the already shared focus feelings. The children then guess which feeling was being shared.

2. Song Squeezers:

Song Squeezers are just like *Poem Pushers* except songs are used to express a focus feeling. The whole group could sing a song in anger or sadness. The facilitator could also play a familiar song in a way which expresses a specific feeling and have the children guess what feeling it is.

3. Show Stoppers:

Show Stoppers are short plays or scenes created by the children to act out one of the focus feelings. These plays or scenes can be as short as two words or as long as ten minutes.

11. EVALUATION INSTRUMENTS:

At the close of each session, an *Evaluation Instrument* is presented for facilitators to assess the effectiveness of the sessions.

12. CULMINATING EXPERIENCE: THE FEELING FAIR

The Feeling Fair, which is presented at the end of the program, provides both a celebration for the completion of the eighteen sessions and an excellent review and sharing experience.

Summary

We have discussed the importance of an accepting atmosphere and a supportive environment for the exploration of children's feelings. The role of the leader was defined as that of a facilitator—a person who provides opportunities for growth and change. The focus of the entire program is on the children—helping them to build positive self-images. through awareness and understanding of their feelings.

You will find each session organized by key elements in the same order as we have introduced these elements to you. While we hope each session will contain sufficient instructions and suggestions for the successful implementation of the activities, you may want to return to this introductory section from time to time to review the information presented here.

You, as the facilitator, can make this program successful if you remember to provide a sound and supportive environment for the children to *explore* and to *own* their feelings.

unit one

happy feelings

To begin to help children to explore feelings and to grow in the area of positive self-image, it is best to start in a positive manner. While this program is designed to help children explore a wide variety of feelings, this initial unit emphasizes happy feelings and the sharing of those feelings with others.

In order to be prepared for the activities contained in this unit, you may wish to assemble the materials needed in the first three sessions at this time.

SESSION ONE: HAPPY FEELINGS ARE OKAY

Board and chalk or large paper and marking pen; clay; *Reinforcement Activity: Happy Clown.*

Happy Clown: A large, happy clown can be drawn or painted on cardboard, the blackboard or any suitable surface. The clown should have a number of circles to be colored. In sessions two and three, as they share happy feelings, the children color in a circle. The number of coloring turns and circles are determined by the number of children involved. At the end of session three, all the circles are colored and the reward is shared.

SESSION TWO: SHARED HAPPINESS

Consturction paper; scissors; glue; magazines or manila paper; paint or crayons; *Reinforcement Activity: Happy Clown.*

SESSION THREE: FREE TO FEEL HAPPY

Board; chalk; *Reinforcement Activity: Happy Clown; Reinforcement Sticker:* I am responsible for my happy feelings (or materials to make them); *Suggested Reward*: A container of punch, juice or lemonade is shared by the group. Each person dips out a small amount of drink into an individual cup and shares a happy thought before drinking.

Session One:
HAPPY FEELINGS ARE OKAY

Rationale

"Happiness is contagious."

K. Morrison

Goals

To identify and accept happy feelings.
To share happy feelings.
To understand it is all right to feel happy.

Materials

Board and chalk or large paper and marking pen; clay; *Reinforcement Activity: Happy Clown.*

Thought Catcher:
"OLD KING COLE"

Old King Cole
Was a merry old soul,
And a merry old soul was he;
He called for his pipe,
And he called for his bowl,
And he called for his fiddlers three.

Process Activities

A. DISCUSSION STARTERS:

1. Why do you think Old King Cole was so merry?
2. Are there *special* people or things that you like when you are happy?
3. Do the words "merry" and "happy" mean the same?
4. How do you look when you are happy?
5. How do you behave when you are happy?
6. When you are happy, are the other people around you usually happy too?
7. What makes you happy in school?
8. What makes you happy at home?
9. How do you feel when you are happy?
10. Do you feel better when you are happy?

B. HAPPY LIST:

Children and facilitator develop a list of things that make people happy.

C. CLAY SHAPES:

Children and facilitator make something (a shape from clay) that helps them feel happy. Older children can be encouraged to make a symbolic shape which represents how they feel when they are happy.

D. SHARING TIME:

Clay shapes are shared. The facilitator encourages the sharing of the objects and how each object relates to that child's happiness.

E. CLOSING QUESTIONS:

Facilitator asks: "Is it okay to feel happy?" "What are some things that make people happy?" "What makes you happy?" All answers are accepted.

F. INTRODUCTION OF REINFORCEMENT ACTIVITY:

Facilitator explains the *Reinforcement Activity: Happy Clown.* Children and facilitator are asked to share a happy feeling with someone before the next session.

The shared happiness can be limited to a specific time period. At the end of sessions two and three these shared happy feelings are explained and circles can be colored in on the *Happy Clown.*

Curricular-Related Activities

A. ART:

Draw yourself as King or Queen and surround yourself with things that make you happy.

B. DRAMA:

Act out being King or Queen—call for what you want as Old King Cole did. Then everyone shares feelings bout being the King or the Queen.

C. GYM (Physical Education):

One person is King or Queen. The King or Queen then names three things that would make that person happy. Other people choose secretly which of the three things they would want. Then the King or Queen stands at one end of the room and the other persons stand at the opposite end.

The King or Queen yells out the name of one of the three things. Anyone who has chosen to be that thing must run to the other end to be safe. The King or Queen tags as many runners as possible. Those caught are added to the King or Queen's Court and participate in the tagging of others.

Those safe return to the original line and the game continues until one person is left. The person left then becomes the new King or Queen.

D. FORMING (Language Arts):

Children are asked to write a fairy tale in which they are King or Queen and they call for three things which would please them. They should also tell what happens when they get their wishes. Stories related to this theme can be read aloud by the children to the rest of the group.

Pretending Time

A minimum of 15-20 minutes should be allocated for this activity.

A. READY-SET-GO:

The children get into comfortable positions. These positions can be either sitting or lying, but far enough apart so that no one is touching anyone else.

The facilitator then says: "Please get comfortable and just enjoy being quiet for a few moments. . . Now, just relax; it is all right to do nothing. . . ." (More time, indicated by . . . should be taken.)

B. PRETENDING:

The facilitator says: "I would like you to pretend you are a King or a Queen and are sitting on a beautiful golden throne. . . Now, as King or Queen, you can have anything you want, so please ask a servant to bring you something special. . . What did you ask for? . . . What did you get? . . . Look closely at it. . . Spend some time with it. . . Enjoy yourself. . . Now, it is time to give this thing back. . . How do you feel about this? . . . Say 'goodbye' to this thing. . . And, now, stop pretending and slowly become yourself. . . ."

C. STOP-LOOK-LISTEN:

The facilitator follows by saying: "Now, I want you to get down from your throne and stop pretending. . . You have stopped pretending, just relax. . . Be quiet. . . Look back at the pretending. . . Think about it for a moment and listen to others. . . ."

D. REFLECTIONS:

The facilitator may ask the following questions of the group as a whole, remembering there are no right or wrong answers.

1. Did you enjoy pretending?
2. What part did you like best?
3. What was the hardest part?
4. As King or Queen, how did you look?
5. How did you feel as King or Queen?
6. What did you ask for that was special?
7. Did you get what you asked for?
8. Describe what you got and what you did with it.
9. How did it feel when you had to give the special thing back?
10. Can you have this special thing in real life?

Fable:
"THE GOOSE AND THE GOLDEN EGGS"

A man had a great good fortune to own a marvelous goose—every day it laid a golden egg. the man was growing rich but the more he got, the more he wanted. Making up his mind to have the whole treasure at once, he killed the goose. But, when he killed the goose and cut her open, instead of finding a horde of golden eggs, he found that she was just like any other goose.

FOLLOW-UP QUESTIONS:

1. Why do you think the rich man wanted more eggs?
2. Do you ever think you would be happier if you had *more* of somethings? Please explain.
3. What would you like to have more of than you now have?
4. Are you usually happy when you get something you don't get too often?
5. Did you ever have too much of a good thing?
6. How come the man was not satisfied with what he had?
7. Do you think that people need things in order to be happy?

Supplemental Activities

SENSE STRETCHERS:

1. Eyes:

Children bring in an object or a picture that helps make them feel happy. They are asked to share the objects and the reasons for their choices.

2. Ears:

The children express words that are happy words to them. Also, happy sounds may be shared.

3. Nose:

The children are requested to bring in items that produce smells that help them feel happy. Examples might be an old doll, cookies, perfume, bubble gum, paste or pizza sauce.

4. Tongue:

The facilitator makes a picture of a *Happy Tongue* and children paste pictures of food they like on it. Also, the names of favorite foods can be written on the *Happy Tongue.*

P. S. (POST SCRIPT) ACTIVITIES:

1. Poem Pushers:

The children are asked to share a favorite poem or make up a happy rhyme.

2. Song Squeezers:

The facilitator leads the children in some happy songs with lots of happy faces and happy movements being part of the singing.

3. Show Stoppers:

The children are asked to choose a character from a poem or story and pretend to be that character telling why they are happy.

Evaluation

SELF-EVALUATION PROGRESS CHECK

	Extremely	*Very*	*Reasonably*	*Slightly*	*Not at All*
1. How comfortable was I during the session?					
2. Were the children comfortable during the session?					
3. Were the children willing to share feelings freely?					
4. How well did the children accept the feelings of others?					
5. How accepting was I of the children's responses?					
6. How eager were the children to participate?					
7. How well did the children listen?					
8. Was the environment supportive and safe?					
9. How effective were the questions that I asked?					
10. How interested did the group appear to be?					

Session Two:
SHARED HAPPINESS

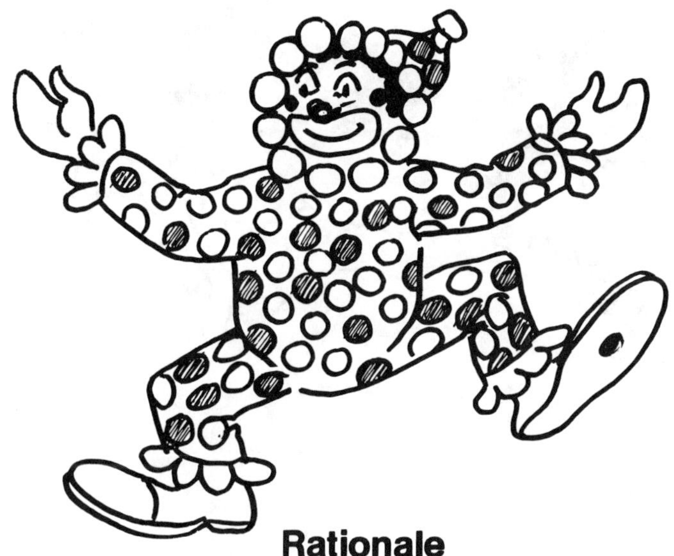

Rationale

"Happiness is an experience shared."

K. Morrison

Goals

To review happy feelings.
To expand happy feelings.
To claim happy feelings.
To introduce the idea of being responsible for feelings.

Materials

Construction paper; scissors; glue; magazines or manila paper; paint or crayons; *Reinforcement Activity: Happy Clown* (see page 22).

Thought Catcher:
"HEY DIDDLE DIDDLE"

Hey diddle, diddle,
The cat and the fiddle,
The cow jumped over the moon;
The litte dog laughed,
To see such sport,
And the dish ran away with the spoon.

Process Activities

A. DISCUSSION STARTERS:

1. How come everyone in this rhyme seems to be having fun being silly and doing unusual things?
2. Do you ever laugh like the dog did at your own or your friends' funny actions?
3. Is there a difference between laughing *with* a person instead of laughing *at* a person?
4. Is it sometimes more fun to do things with others and then talk about what you did?
5. With whom do you most like to share happy feelings?

B. HAPPY MEMORIES:

Children and facilitator identify and share a remembered happiness of another individual in the group. The following words can be used as a guide: "I remember that________________ helps ________________ feel happy."

C. HAPPY POSTERS:

Children and facilitator make a collage or a picture of things that help them feel happy.

D. SHARING TIME:

Children and facilitator share their posters.

E. REINFORCEMENT ACTIVITY:

Happy Clown: Children and facilitator share happy feelings and color the happy clown's circles (see page 22).

F. CLOSING QUESTIONS:

The facilitator asks: "Is it okay to feel happy?" "Who makes you feel happy?" All answers are accepted.

Curricular-Related Activities

A. ART:

Draw something really silly, funny or unusual—something that makes *you* laugh. Discuss pictures that make people laugh and generally what people laugh about in pictures.

B. DRAMA:

Choose some friends and act out a silly scene from a play for others. Discuss what being silly does for people, both positive and negative aspects should be explored.

C. GYM (Physical Education):

Relay Race. From a given starting point to a home base:

First—run, pick up a stick, play and hum a chosen, common song;

Second—jump over an object; Third—laugh ten belly laughs; and Fourth—grab an object, like a spoon, and run home.

D. FORMING (Language Arts):

Children may enjoy writing riddles, limericks or funny stories. They can be shared orally or displayed for all to read. Discuss humorous writing and its place in literature.

Pretending Time

A minimum of 15-20 minutes should be allocated for this activity.

A. READY-SET-GO:

The children get into comfortable positions. Then the facilitator says: "Please relax. . . Be very quiet. . . It is okay just to do nothing. . . ."

B. PRETENDING:

The facilitator says: "Today, I want you to become a Giggle—a little, bright, happy Giggle. . . How do you look? . . . How do you feel? . . . As a Giggle, do whatever you want to, go wherever you want to, enjoy yourself. . . Now, begin to grow from a Giggle to become a great big Laugh. . . How have you changed? . . . How do you look now? . . How do you feel? . . . Now, fill the world with your laughter. . . What do you see? . . . What do you feel? . . Everything and everyone is happy . . . And, you can now slowly become yourself, but bring along with you some happiness. . . ."

C. STOP-LOOK-LISTEN:

The facilitator says: "Now, stop pretending. . . Let the happiness you feel slowly get smaller and smaller. . . You are no longer a Laugh, but a Giggle. . . And now I want you to go from being a Giggle to being you. . . You are now yourself. . . You are relaxed. You are enjoying just being where you are and what you are doing. . . It is okay. . . Now that you have stopped pretending, think about how the pretending was and listen to what others have to say."

D. REFLECTIONS:

The facilitator may ask the following questions, expecting nothing, accepting everything.

1. Did you enjoy the pretending?
2. What part did you enjoy the most?
3. What part did you not enjoy?
4. How did you feel being a giggle?
5. How did you look?
6. Describe how you looked when you changed from a giggle to a big laugh.
7. Tell how the world looked when it was all happy.
8. How did you feel when you went from being a laugh to a giggle to being you?
9. How do you make the real world happier?

Fable:
"THE FISHERMEN AND THE TUNA"

Some fishermen had gone out to fish and after struggling for a long time without catching a thing, were just sitting dejectedly in their boat. At that point, a tuna, swimming along in full flight with a great swish, leapt blindly into the boat. The fishermen pounced upon the tuna, rowed back to the city and sold their catch.

FOLLOW-UP QUESTIONS:

1. What activity do you like to do with others?
2. How do you think the fishermen felt when they did not catch any fish?
3. How do you feel when you try hard and still are not successful?
4. Is it possible, sometimes, to try *too* hard?
5. How do you think the men felt when the tuna jumped into the boat ?
6. How do you think the men shared their feelings after the tuna jumped into the boat?

Supplemental Activities

SENSE STRETCHERS:

Some suggested *Sense Stretchers* that might go with this session are:

1. Eyes:

Children share something or some place in nature that seeing it or remembering it brings happy thoughts.

2. Ears:

The children are requested to make happy sounds—not words. Sounds like a favorite song, melody, a giggle, a laugh, a hiccup and so forth.

3. Nose:

The children are taken on a field trip to a bakery, or other such food producing business, and allowed to smell all the happy smells. (If necessary, this can be an imaginary trip.)

4. Tongue:

While at the bakery, or other appropriate setting, the children are given some samples of the happy smells to eat. (If an imaginary trip was taken, a treat can still be shared.)

P. S. (POST SCRIPT) ACTIVITIES:

1. Poem Pushers:

The facilitator reads several happy poems and the children are asked to act them out.

2. Song Squeezers:

The children choose certain songs that help make them feel happy when they sing them.

3. Show Stoppers:

Poems are acted out with the children making up their own happy ending. An example of this would be *Old Mother Hubbard* who finds a bone for her dog, but also a new hat for herself.

Evaluation

PERSONAL NOTES

The purpose of the personal notes is to allow and aid reflection. It is important for the facilitator to look back and recapitulate what has occurred thus far and to write down thoughts, feelings and experiences which have happened durring the sessions.

Frequently, progress is difficult to detect while actively engaged in the session. The personal notes will help promote and provide perceivable progress.

Session Three: Free to Feel Happy

Rationale

"Often the admission to happiness is permission."

K. Morrison

Goals

To identify happy feelings.
To identify responsibility for one's own feelings.

Materials

Board; chalk; *Reinforcement Activity: Happy Clown; Reinforcement Sticker* (or materials to make them); *Suggested Reward.*

Thought Catcher:
"MARY HAD A LITTLE LAMB"

Mary had a little lamb,
Its fleece was white as snow;
And everywhere that Mary went,
The lamb was sure to go.

It followed her to school one day,
Which was against the rules;
It made the children laugh and play,
To see a lamb in school.

Process Activities

A. DISCUSSION STARTERS:

1. When others do things that are against the rules, does that sometimes strike your funny bone?
2. Can you share such a time with us now?
3. How do you feel when you laugh at a time when others think you shouldn't laugh?
4. How come the children laughed when the lamb followed Mary to school?
5. Is it okay to laugh sometimes even though others might not think it's all right?

B. REINFORCEMENT ACTIVITY:

Happy Clown: Children and facilitator share happy thoughts and/or experiences and color in the happy clown's circles (see page 22).

C. ROBOT TALK:

The facilitator asks: "What is a robot?" "Who controls a robot?"

D. ROBOT GAME:

Children pretend they are robots and the facilitator gives them various commands. Then each child experiences being the controller of the other robots.

E. SHARING TIME:

The children and the facilitator share the feelings and thoughts they had being robots and controllers.

F. QUESTION TIME:

The facilitator asks: "Do you feel like a robot sometimes?" "When you do, who controls you?" "How do you feel when you're the controller?"

G. REINFORCEMENT STICKER:

I am responsible for my happiness. The facilitator hands out stickers or material and directions for making them (see page 22).

H. SUGGESTED REWARD:

A container of punch, juice or lemonade is shared by the group. Each person dips out a small amount of drink into an individual cup and shares a happy thought before drinking.

Curricular-Related Activities

A. ART:

The children draw funny bones and fill them with things that make them laugh. Discuss what a funny bone really is and if everyone has one.

B. DRAMA:

Act out *Mary Had a Little Lamb.* Check out the feelings of the various characters at the end. It might be particularly interesting to find out which characters were most fun to act out.

C. GYM (Physical Education):

The gàme, *Pass the Funny Bone*, is played by everyone standing in a circle with their hands behind their backs. One person walks the outside of the circle with the funny bone. Just before putting it into the hands of one person, the person who is "it" laughs out loud and then runs around the circle being chased by the person with the bone. The person who is "it" must get back to the open space without getting caught.

D. FORMING (Language Arts):

Children are asked to write a science fiction story in which there are robots trying to become free, happy human beings. What happens and how they are finally freed can be shared orally or a large book of science fiction stories can be made for all to read privately.

Pretending Time

A minimum of 15-20 minutes should be allocated for this activity.

A. READY-SET-GO:

The children get into comfortable positions. Then the facilitator says: "Please relax. . . It is good being quiet. . . Feeling comfortable. . . ."

B. PRETENDING:

The facilitator says: "Today, I want you to become a little, wrapped box. . . There is a lot of paper and string wrapped around you. . . How does this feel? . . . What do you think about? . . . What do you want to do? . . . Suddenly, someone comes near and begins to gently untie the string. . . How does this feel? . . . More of the string is loosened until, finally, you are stringless. . . Now, the paper is slowly being removed. . . What are you thinking? . . . Feeling? . . . And now, you are more free. . . What is it like? . . . What do you do? . . . What do you feel? . . . Enjoy for a moment this freedom. . . Now, you are gently being opened and your self is set free into the world. . . What do you look like? . . . What do you do? . . . How do you feel?"

C. STOP-LOOK-LISTEN:

The facilitator says: "Stop pretending. . . Being free is wonderful. . . Enjoy this for a moment more. . . Now, I want you to think back to the open box. . . What was it like? . . . Share your thoughts with others and also listen to the views of others."

D. REFLECTIONS:

The facilitator may ask the following questions, remembering all answers are okay.

1. Is this kind of pretending getting easier?
2. Are you learning more about this kind of pretending each time?
3. Do you feel it is fun when you do this kind of pretending?
4. What was it like being all wrapped up as a box?
5. What did you think and/or feel about the person unwrapping you?
6. What was it like being all unwrapped?
7. How did you feel when the box was opened?
8. Has anyone in real life helped make you feel more free?

Fable:
"THE ASTRONOMER"

An astronomer was in the habit of going out regularly in the evening to observe the stars. Once as he was strolling through the outskirts of the town with his attention completely fixed on the heavens, he fell into a well before he knew what was happening to him. While he was howling and shouting, a passerby who heard his pitiful tones came up and, as soon as he found out what had happened, remarked, "My good fellow, while you're trying to watch things in the heavens, you don't even see things on earth."

FOLLOW-UP QUESTIONS:

1. What do you think the astronomer was thinking about when he fell into the well?
2. Do you ever feel yourself not paying attention to something and then getting into trouble?
3. Have you ever missed something really good because you were thinking about or doing another thing?

Supplemental Activities

SENSE STRETCHERS:

Some suggested *Sense Stretchers* that might be appropriate with this session are:

1. Eyes:

The facilitator shows a series of pictures or slides and asks the children what helps make them feel happy in that picture or slide.

2. Ears:

The facilitator reads a short story or poem and the children pick out happy words, thoughts or events.

3. Nose:

The facilitator shares various items like pepper, cocoa, flowers, soap, an old book, jam and so forth with the children. As the item is passed and smelled, the children are asked to share any happy memories they might have with a similar item.

4. Tongue:

A happy meal can be planned by the children. Everyone brings a favorite food and shares it. Happy plates, cups and napkins can be made by children for this *Happy Feast.*

P. S. (POST SCRIPT) ACTIVITIES:

1. Poem Pushers:

The children may wish to pantomime *Old King Cole, Hey Diddle Diddle* or *Mary Had a Little Lamb* while the rest of the children guess which one is being acted out.

2. Song Squeezers:

A child is asked to hum a song in a happy way. The other children try to guess the name of the song and the person who guesses it has the next turn to do the same thing.

3. Show Stoppers:

The children share funny stories or formulate television programs which make them happy.

Evaluation

PROGRAM-PROGRESS CHECK

To be used by facilitator or children

1. What I liked *best* about the Happy Feelings Sessions was ______________________________
2. What I liked *least* about the Happy Feelings Sessions was ______________________________
3. What I wanted to happen in these Happy Feelings Sessions which *never* came about was ______________ ______________________________
4. During the Happy Feelings Sessions, I wish I would have ______________________________
5. My overall *feelings* about the Happy Feelings Sessions are ______________________________

unit two

angry feelings

Feeling good about ourselves is important to the development of positive self-images, but we do not always feel good about ourselves or do we always feel happy.

The next sessions, therefore, deal with anger and how we learn to be responsible for personal negative feelings. It is unrealistic to assume that anger does not exist, but it is not unrealistic to assume that anger can be handled responsibly and used to help develop a positive self-image.

The materials needed for the next three sessions, including the *Reinforcement Activity, Suggested Reward* and the *Reinforcement Sticker* are presented here for your preparation.

SESSION FOUR: MEETING ANGER FACE TO FACE

Reinforcement Activity: Angry Pie. This pie can be made of any variety of material. It should provide room for shared angry feelings and experiences to be written and, perhaps, it should be colorful in nature. A specific number of places on which to write can be made according to the number of participants, remembering that there are two days of sharing.

SESSION FIVE: LETTING OFF STEAM

Four or five balloons; *Reinforcement Activity: Angry Pie.*

SESSION SIX: ANGER—FRIEND OR FOE?

Reinforcement Activity: Angry Pie; Reinforcement Sticker: I am responsible for my angry feelings (or materials to make them); *Suggested Reward: Privilege Pie.* Each child receives a slice of the *Angry Pie.* This is then traded in after the children individually share how they might have controlled one of the angry feelings on their slice of pie. This slice of *Angry Pie* is traded in for a slice of real pie or a slice of a *Privilege Pie.* The *Privilege Pie* is made up of extra privileges such as ten extra minutes of reading, teacher's helper, ten points on the next math test and so forth. This pie can be made up by the facilitator or by the class.

Angry Pie

Session Four:
Meeting Anger Face to Face

Rationale

"Anger once faced is no longer an enemy and may become a friend."

K. Morrison

Goals

To identify angry feelings.
To claim angry feelings.
To share angry feelings.
To claim responsibility over anger.
To share feelings.

Materials

Reinforcement Activity: Angry Pie.

Thought Catcher:
"OLD WOMAN WHO LIVED IN A SHOE"

There was an old woman who lived in a shoe,
She had so many children she didn't know what to do;
She gave them some broth without any bread,
She whipped them all soundly and sent them to bed.

Process Activities

A. DISCUSSION STARTERS:

1. Did the woman in the shoe get angry because she didn't love her children? What could be her reasons for getting angry?
2. Do things ever pile up around you and you get angry at someone else because of *other* things?
3. Do you ever get so angry that you do not know what to do?
4. What makes you most angry? How do you act then?
5. Is it all right for you to get angry?
6. Is it anger that causes people to have problems, or, how do they act when they are angry?
7. Can you control your angry behavior? How?

B. ANGER REMEMBERED:

Children are asked to get into a comfortable position and a few minutes are taken to relax and have a quiet time.

Then they are asked to imagine a scene real or make-believe where they find themselves angry. Two or three minutes can be given for this.

The children are then asked to slowly stop imagining and to share with others.

C. SHARING TIME:

The facilitator asks the children to share, answering the following questions if they would like.

1. What did you imagine?
2. What made you angry?
3. Can you describe the angry feeling?
4. What did you do when you felt angry?

D. RESPONSIBILITY CIRCLE:

A circle is formed. One by one, the children step forward into the center and say: "I am responsible for myself. I can chose to be __________ . I can ______________ ." (jump, hop, laugh, smile, cry and so fourth.) Everyone repeats the expressed control and then another child is chosen by the one in the center.

E. QUESTION TIME:

The facilitator asks the following questions orally and the children answer silently think about the questions:

1. How do you feel when you are responsible for yourself?
2. In the imagining, who was responsible for your anger?
3. In that imagining, how was your anger controlled?
4. Did you feel responsible for parts of your anger during the imagining?

F. MORE SHARING TIME:

These open-ended questions can be used to start an open sharing of thoughts about anger:

1. Angry Feelings are________________________________ .
2. When I am angry, I feel like _________________________.
3. When I am angry, I want to __________________________.
4. When someone is angry at me, I feel _________________.

G. INTRODUCTION OF REINFORCEMENT ACTIVITY:

The facilitator introduces the *Angry Pie* and explains the rules of the activity and the reward.

Curricular-Related Activities

A. ART:

Bring an old shoe. Decorate it with pictures, words, things that make you angry.

B. DRAMA:

Act out the story of the *Old Woman Who Lived in a Shoe* and her children. Check out all the feelings of the characters before, during and after the short drama.

C. GYM (Physical Education):

One person is the "Old Woman." That child stands at the end of the room and calls out commands like: "Come all my children that have blue eyes," or, "Come all my children that wear shoes." If others fit the description, they must run to the goal behind the Old Woman before being tagged. All persons tagged are put in an imaginary shoe. The last person to be caught gets to be the Old Woman next time.

D. FORMING (Language Arts):

Children are asked to write a story as one of the Old Woman's children. They are to describe themselves (age, height, hair color and so forth), and tell how they feel about living with the old woman. A discussion could follow relating elements of literature and the focused feeling.

Pretending Time

A minimum of 15-20 minutes should be allocated for this activity.

A. READY-SET-GO:

The children get into comfortable positions. Then the facilitator says: "Please spend a few moments enjoying the sound of a quiet room. . . Feel comfortable. . . Now, please imagine a swing, swinging gently back and forth. . . Back and forth. . . ."

B. PRETENDING:

The facilitator says: "Now, let the swing slowly slow down to a stop. . . I want you to pretend you are the old shoe where the Old Woman and her children live. . . What do you look like? . . . What are you made of? . . . What kind of condition are you in? . . . How does the Old Woman treat you? . . . What kind of sounds do you hear as the old shoe? . . . What is the nicest thing that ever happened to you? . . . If you could say something to the Old Woman, what would it be? . . . To the children? . . . Now, it is night, all is quiet in the old shoe. . . Everyone is asleep. . . How do you feel? . . . What do you think? . . ."

C. STOP-LOOK-LISTEN:

The facilitator says: "It is so quiet. . . There are no sounds. . . Stop pretending. . . Now that you have stopped pretending to be the old shoe, think how you felt being the shoe. . . What was it like? . . . What do you think it was like for others? . . . Listen."

D. REFLECTIONS:

The facilitator may ask the following questions:

1. What was it like being the Old Woman's shoe?
2. What did you look like?
3. How did you feel being that shoe?
4. Would you rather pretend being a different shoe? If so, which one and how come?
5. What did you say to the Old Woman?
6. What did you say to the children?
7. How did you feel when everyone was asleep and it was quiet?
8. Do you ever feel that someone is angry with you in real life?
9. When do you get angry with someone or something? What or who?
10. If you were the Old Woman, how would you treat the old shoe?

Fable:
"THE BOY AND THE WOLF"

A Boy who was employed to tend sheep was often bored with the task. To create a little excitement, he would rush toward the village crying "wolf! wolf!" When the villagers came with clubs and pitchforks to help him, they found nothing. This seemed such a good sport that a few days later the Boy cried out again and once more the people ran to help him.

One day a wolf actually did come out of the forest. But, this time when the Boy cried "wolf! wolf!" the villagers thought he was playing his tricks again and refused to stir. Meanwhile, the sheep were at the mercy of the Wolf, who enjoyed a hearty meal.

FOLLOW-UP QUESTIONS:

1. Can you imagine how the men felt after being tricked by the boy?
2. Have you ever intentionally caused someone to be angry?
3. Do you think being bored might cause someone to do something to make others angry?
4. If people are angry with you, are they usually willing to help you?
5. Is it okay to "play" or pretend you are feeling something that you are not?

Supplemental Activities

SENSE STRETCHERS:

1. Eyes:

The children find pictures or draw pictures of angry faces. An extension of this activity might be guessing or telling why that face is angry.

2. Ears:

The children attempt to make angry sounds that people or animals make. An example is an angry growling bear standing on hind legs pawing angrily at the air.

3. Nose:

The children create an imaginary meal that is made up of foods having strong smells. Examples of this might be spinach salad, liver, an old tuna sandwich and so forth.

4. Tongue:

The children are asked to share any experience where they had to eat something that they did not like and how angry they felt about it.

P. S. (POST SCRIPT) ACTIVITIES:

1. Poem Pushers:

The children can read or recite any poem of their choice in an angry voice and manner.

2. Song Squeezers:

The children choose their favorite songs and individually or in groups they sing the songs in very angry voices.

3. Show Stoppers:

The facilitator sets up a simple scene which is first acted out with kindness. Then the second time one of the actors is asked to be angry. The audience then re-acts to both scenes.

Evaluation

SELF-EVALUATION PROGRESS CHECK

	Extremely	*Very*	*Reasonably*	*Slightly*	*Not at All*
1. How comfortable was I during the session?					
2. Were the children comfortable during the session?					
3. Were the children willing to share feelings freely?					
4. How well did the children accept the feelings of others?					
5. How accepting was I of the children's responses?					
6. How eager were the children to participate?					
7. How well did the children listen?					
8. Was the environment supportive and safe?					
9. How effective were the questions that I asked?					
10. How interested did the group appear to be?					

Session Five: Letting off Steam

Angry Pie

Rationale

"The more ways we have to express our anger, the better chance we have of holding on to our self control."

Adele Faber and Elaine Mazlish

Goals

To identify and claim sources of anger.
To demonstrate various ways of expressing anger.
To question personal role in anger.
To act out anger in various ways.
To claim responsibility for anger in self.
To claim responsibility over angry feelings.

Materials

Four or five balloons; *Reinforcement Activity: Angry Pie.*

Thought Catcher:
"CROSS PATCH"

Cross patch
Draw the latch
Sit by the fire and spin;
Take a cup
And drink it up
And call your neighbors in.

Process Activities

A. DISCUSSION STARTERS:

1. Can you guess some reasons for being called "Cross Patch?" What kind of behavior would a "Cross Patch" demonstrate?
2. The rhyme suggests that Cross Patch call in some neighbors; have you ever felt less cross after you have shared your feelings with someone else?
3. Is being cross a better way to share anger than some other ways?
4. If it is okay to share happy feelings, is it okay to share angry feelings?
5. Are there differences between grown-ups being cross and children being cross? If there are some differences, could you share them?

B. REINFORCEMENT ACTIVITY:

A list is made of things that lately helped us feel angry. These ideas are used to fill in some of the pieces of the *Angry Pie.*

C. BALLOON EXERCISE:

The facilitator tells a short story about a child or an adult who encounters one frustration after another until blowing up in anger. As the story is being told, the facilitator blows up a balloon a little each time the child or adult gets angry. The balloon should explode when the person in the story does.

The story is then retold briefly with the balloon getting almost full and then let go so that it flies around the room. This demonstrates one different way of handling anger—although still uncontrolled.

The story is then retold a third time with the balloon being blown up as the person in the story becomes angry, but this time the air is let out right away or at least by the second or third small blow. This story demonstrates the value of identifying and expressing angry feelings as soon as possible.

D. QUESTION TIME:

The facilitator explains that we are all like balloons and can fill ourselves up with anger until we blow up or we can fill with anger until we act uncontrolled, or we can express our anger when it occurs and is small enought to handle or control.

1. What kind of angry balloon are you? Why?
2. What kind of angry balloon do you want to be around? Why?

E. ANGRY ROLE PLAYING:

The facilitator and the children act out angry scenes using the angry list in the *Reinforcement Activity: Angry Pie* as the basis. Each scene is acted out three times to depict the three types of balloons. (Scenes should be short and simple.)

F. SHARING TIME:

Time is spent talking about:

1. Children's feelings as various balloons.
2. Kinds of balloons they would like to be.
3. Verbal and nonverbal ways of expressing desired expressions of anger.

Curricular-Related Activities

A. ART:

Draw a cup. Decorate one side. Draw or write things that make you cross on the other side. Choose a partner to share your cup and vice versa.

B. DRAMA:

Act out the rhyme and the check feelings out after the short scene.

C. GYM (Physical Education):

Someone is chosen to be "Cross Patch." This person sits with back to group at the far end of the room. The other children quietly sneak toward Cross Patch. When Cross Patch thinks they are close enough to catch, Cross Patch jumps up, acts angry and chases them back to the starting point. Those caught are out—a new Cross Patch results when a child is successful in sneaking up and touching Cross Patch on the back.

D. FORMING (Language Arts):

Children are asked to write a story about their most horrible day (real or pretend). These stories can be shared. How the days got to be so horrible can be discussed.

Pretending Time

A minimum of 15-20 minutes should be allocated for this activity.

A. READY-SET-GO:

The children are asked to get into comfortable positions. Then the facilitator says: "Please relax. . . Now, let your body sway back and forth, very slowly. . . Rock yourself very gently. . . It is an easy, gentle, slow rocking. . . ."

B. PRETENDING:

The facilitator says: "Now, slowly stop your rocking. . . Come to a slow stop. . . Just relax. . . Now, I want you to see a small dark box. . . Come closer to the box. . . As you come closer, you will notice it says "Anger" on the top. . . Look closely at the box. . . How does it look? . . . What are you feeling? . . . You decide to open the box. . . Slowly, you lift the top. . . Inside the box is something or someone that makes you angry. . . What do you see? . . . What do you do?. . . How do you feel? . . . What do you do next? . . ."

C. STOP-LOOK-LISTEN:

The facilitator says: "Stop pretending; now the angry thing is covered up or gone. . . You can move toward a gentle soft cloud that is not far from you. . . Lie down in this beautiful cloud. . . Get comfortable. . . Think what it was like to be in the cloud. . . Listen to how others felt about the pretending."

D. REFLECTIONS:

The facilitator may ask the following questions:

1. What did the box look like?
2. How did you feel about opening a box filled with anger?
3. What was inside the box?
4. What did you do with the anger you found inside the box?
5. How did you feel about this angry thing?
6. What would you have liked to say to this angry thing?
7. Do you ever feel like you have an angry thing inside you? When?
8. What can you do with angry feelings that are in you?

Fable:
"THE FOX AND THE WOODCUTTER"

A fox in flight from the hunters saw a woodcutter and begged to be concealed. The woodcutter told the fox to go into the hut and hide. Before long the hunters came along and asked the woodcutter whether a fox had passed by. The woodcutter said no, but pointed to where the fox was hidden.

The hunters paid no attention to the woodcutter's gesture but believed what was said. When the fox saw they were gone, it came out and was going off without saying a word. The the woodcutter was angry at the fox for not even saying a word of thanks. The fox replied, "Oh, I should have been grateful enough to you if your actions had agreed with your words."

FOLLOW-UP QUESTIONS:

1. Did someone ever tell you one thing and then do another?
2. How did you feel when that happened?
3. How do you think the fox felt?
4. Do you think that people sometimes say one thing and then act another way?
5. Can you think of a time when you said one thing and then acted another way?

Supplemental Activities

SENSE STRETCHERS:

Some suggested *Sense Stretchers* that might accompany this session are:

1. Eyes:

The children share something they saw that helped make them feel angry.

2. Ears:

A box is provided by the facilitator which is filled with all the angry words that the children can remember. The words can be written out after being expressed or the box can be passed around and the angry words just put into the box. The box containing all the angry words is then thrown away.

3. Nose:

The children describe or bring in items that have a smell they dislike and that help make them angry.

4. Tongue:

The children may bring in food or pictures of food that they dislike the taste of and would be angry if they had to eat.

P. S. (POST SCRIPT) ACTIVITIES:

1. Poem Pushers:

Poems can be read together as a group with angry actions added to emphasize the words.

2. Song Squeezers:

Angry music is played on a piano or record player while children walk around showing angry actions in time to the music.

3. Show Stoppers:

An empty chair is provided for an individual child or a small group to express anger toward someone or something imagined to be in the chair.

Evaluation

PERSONAL NOTES

The purpose of the personal notes is to allow and aid reflection. It is important for the facilitator to look back and recapitulate what has occurred thus far and to write down thoughts, feelings and experiences which have happened during the sessions.

Frequently, progress is difficult to detect while actively engaged in the session. The personal notes will help promote and provide perceivable progress.

Session Six: Anger—Friend or Foe?

Rationale

"Anger without insult remains our only civilized alternative to methods that dehumanize."

Adele Faber and Elaine Maxlish

Goals

To identify and claim angry feelings.
To claim responsibility for angry feelings.

Materials

Reinforcement Activity: Angry Pie; Reinforcement Sticker: I am responsible for my angry feelings (or the materials to make them); *Suggested Reward: Privilege Pie.*

Thought Catcher:
"MISTRESS MARY"

**Mistress Mary, quite contrary,
How does your garden grow?
With silver bells, and cockle shells,
And pretty maids all in a row.**

Process Activities

A. DISCUSSION STARTERS:

1. People who are contrary are those who are cranky, strong-willed and do what they please. Even though Mary was surrounded by beauty, she was contrary. Can you suggest reasons for this?
2. Have you ever had to work hard at staying angry?
3. Are there times when you are contrary?
4. Is it all right to feel and act contrary sometimes?
5. Are other people sometimes contrary, like parents, teachers, brothers or sisters?

B. RE-RUN OF ANGRY VISION:

The facilitator asks the children to get comfortable and relaxed. Then the children are asked to re-run the fantasy they had in the first session, but this time, to take self control over the anger they experienced and act accordingly.

C. SHARING TIME:

The facilitator and the children answer the following questions and other feelings and thoughts:

1. How was the fantasy re-run different?
2. Did you claim some responsibility over your angry feelings?
3. Explain the difference in feelings of anger in the first and the re-run fantasy.
4. Can you now accept more responsibility for your anger?

D. ANGRY WORD PICTURES:

The facilitator and the children answer the following open-ended questions:

1. Unresponsible anger looks like ____________________.
2. Responsible anger looks like ____________________.

3. Unresponsible anger feels like ______________________.
4. Responsible anger feels like ______________________.
5. Unresponsible anger sounds like ______________________.
6. Responsible anger sounds like ______________________.
7. Unresponsible anger tastes like ______________________.
8. Responsible anger tastes like ______________________.
9. Unresponsible anger smells like ______________________.
10. Responsible anger smells like ______________________.
11. Unresponsible anger wants to ______________________.
12. Responsible anger wants to ______________________.

E. REINFORCEMENT ACTIVITY:

The facilitator and the children finish filling in the *Angry Pie* by sharing angry feelings for which they claim some responsibility. When the pie is filled in, each individual is given a slice of the pie.

The slice of pie with various angry experiences on it provides each child with an angry feeling to express and how that experience might be acted on differently with more responsibility. After the sharing, the slice of pie is handed in for a reward.

F. SUGGESTED REWARD:

The slice of *Angry Pie* could be traded in for a slice of real pie or for a slice of a pie of extra privileges. The *Privilege Pie* could include extra reading time, ten points on the next math test, teacher's helper and so forth. The privileges can be chosen by the facilitator or by the class at an earlier time.

G. REINFORCEMENT STICKER:

I am responsible for my angry feelings. The angry control stickers are handed out or materials and instructions to make them. (see page 75)

Curricular-Related Activities

A. ART:

Have a group project of making a garden of beautiful flowers—each with a reason to give up angry feelings written on them.

B. DRAMA:

Be the flowers in Mary's garden and have Mary come and be contrary. Talk back and forth. Check all feelings.

C. GYM (Physical Education):

Mistress Mary is chosen and all the pretty maids line up on one end of the room, the gentlemen on the other. When Mistress Mary feels contrary, she yells " RUN ! " and the girls try to run to the boys without being tagged. If tagged, they are out. After all are tagged, the remaining one becomes Mistress Mary. Then the boys try to get to the girls' starting point.

D. FORMING (Language Arts):

The children are given a flower from Mistress Mary's garden and are asked to write what it is like to be a flower and be cared for by Mary. The flower can be taken home or a bouquet is made for all to enjoy.

Pretending Time

A minimum of 15-20 minutes should be allocated for this activity.

A. READY-SET-GO:

The children are asked to get into comfortable positions. Then the facilitator says: "Please get comfortable. . . Slowly rock back and forth. . . Enjoy the feeling of rocking back and forth."

B. PRETENDING:

The facilitator says: "Now, slowly stop rocking. . . Just quietly be relaxed. . . Today I want you to imagine several different things. Each time we imagine seeing something it will be angry and then not angry. First, let's imagine a large tree being very angry. . . What does it do? . . . How do you feel about this tree? . . Now the tree becomes calm, not angry. . . How does it look? . . How do you feel? . . . Now we are going to see an angry bug. . . How does it act? . . . How do you feel?. . . Now the bug becomes calm, not angry. . . How do you feel about it? . . . Now I want you to think about something that makes *you* angry. . . Begin to get angrier and angrier. . . What do you do? . . . How do you feel? . . . Now find a friend to share your angry feeling with. . . Become calm and quiet now. . . You are no longer angry. . . ."

C. STOP-LOOK-LISTEN:

The facilitator says: "You are quiet. . . You feel no anger. . . Just relax. . . Enjoy doing nothing. . . nothing at all. . . Think back about the pretending and share your feelings. . . Listen to others. . . ."

D. REFLECTIONS:

The facilitator may ask the following questions:

1. Can you describe the tree when it was angry?
2. What did the tree look like when it wasn't angry?
3. How did you feel about the tree when it was angry and then not angry?
4. Describe your angry bug.
5. Did you want to say or do anything to the bug?
6. When the bug was not angry, how did you feel?
7. What do you get angry about?
8. What do you do with your angry feelings?
9. How did your friend react to your angry feelings?
10. In real life, how do you show and share your angry feelings?

Fable:
"THE DOLPHINS AND THE MINNOW"

The dolphins and the whales were fighting with one another. When their quarrel became very violent, a minnow swam up and tried to separate them. One of the dolphins turned to the minnow and said, "Thanks, but we'd rather die fighting one another than have you as a mediator."

FOLLOW-UP QUESTIONS:

1. Can you think of a time when you saw others quarrel and then a fight started?
2. How come people quarrel?
3. Is it all right to quarrel sometimes?
4. How do you think a person knows when it is all right or not all right to interfere when others are quarreling?
5. Is it okay for someone to interfere if that person is a teacher?

Supplemental Activities

SENSE STRETCHERS:

1. Eyes:

The children are asked to close their eyes and see what anger looks like with their "mind's eye."

2. Ears:

The children are given the opportunity to say angry words into a tape recorder. This is then played back and reactions to all that anger is shared. (Save this tape for use in session eighteen.)

3. Nose:

The children and the facilitator make up a smelly story told about a child who spends a day being very angry because of a whole list of icky smells faced that day. The story can progress from getting up in the morning to going to bed at night.

4. Tongue:

The children and the facilitator talk about angry tongues. What they might say, what they might eat to feel that angry way, what they might do; and what they might do to not taste or give out angry feelings so often.

P. S. (POST SCRIPT) ACTIVITIES:

1. Poem Pushers:

Angry poem characters like *The Old Woman Who Lived in a Shoe, Cross Patch, Mistress Mary*, and the teacher in *Mary had a Little Lamb* are interviewed about why they are angry, what they did with their angry feelings and how they feel now.

2. Song Squeezers:

The children are divided into two groups. A favorite song is sung with anger by one group and then with happiness by the other group. Then they both can attempt to sing their angry and happy versions at the same time.

3. Show Stoppers:

Short, angry scenes are created and presented by small groups of children.

Evaluation

1. What I liked *best* about the Angry Feelings Sessions was
   ____
2. What I liked *least* about the Angry Feelings Sessions was
   ____
3. What I wanted to happen in these Angry Feelings Sessions which *never* came about was ______________
   ____
4. During the Angry Feelings Sessions, I wish I would have
   ____
5. My overall *feelings* about the Angry Feelings Sessions are ______________________________

unit three

sad feelings

It is natural to feel good, to feel anger and also to feel sad. However, as in anger, sad feelings can lead to negative self-images if some element of control is not present. The next sessions deal with sadness and how, if approached appropriately, sad feelings can be a constructive part of positive self-image development.

The materials needed for the next three sessions, including the *Reinforcement Activity, Suggested Reward* and the *Reinforcement Sticker* are presented here for your preparation.

SESSION SEVEN: SADNESS, AN OKAY FEELING

Paint; brushes; paper; *Reinforcement Activity: Sad Sack.* A large paper bag is tacked or hung up. Various small pieces of colored paper are made available for writing sad thoughts. On the two sharing days, the sad thoughts are written and/or shared and then pasted on the bag covering the sad face.

SESSION EIGHT: SHARING SADNESS

Tape recorders or note pads and pencils; *Reinforcement Activity: Sad Sack.*

SESSION NINE: DEALING WITH SADNESS

Role playing cards; board; chalk; *Tear Poster; Reinforcement Activity: Sad Sack; Suggested Reward.* The colorful *Sad Sack* is passed around and each child receives a personal note from the facilitator with an accepting, kind message on it.

Reinforcement Sticker: I am responsible for my sad feelings (or material to make them).

Session Seven:
Sadness, an Okay Feeling

Rationale

"Strong emotions are present in all people. Without feelings, we would not be human."

Leo Buscgalia

Goals

To share sad feelings.
To identify and assume responsibility for sad feelings.

Materials

Paints; brushes; paper: *Reinforcement Activity: Sad Sack.*

Thought Catcher:
"OLD MOTHER HUBBARD"

Old Mother Hubbard
Went to the cupboard
To get her poor dog a bone;
But, when she got there
The cupboard was bare,
And so the poor dog had none.

Process Activities

A. DISCUSSION STARTERS:

1. Can you imagine how Mother Hubbard felt as she looked in her empty cupboard?
2. Have there been times in your life when you had to go without something? How did you feel about that? What did you think?
3. How do you think the dog felt?
4. Do animals have the same feelings as people?
5. When mostly do you feel sad?

B. SADNESS PAINTING:

The children are given paints, brushes and paper They are asked to take a few minutes with their eyes shut to think about sad times in their lives. Then, without speaking to anyone, they paint a picture of a sad time or a picture of how sadness feels.

C. SHARING TIME:

The paintings and feelings of sadness are shared.

D. QUESTION TIME:

1. Sad feelings are ______________________________.
2. When I feel sad, I ____________________________.
3. Other people's sadness helps me feel ______________.
4. When I share sad feelings with ____________________.
5. I can share sad feelings with _____________________.
6. One of the saddest things that happened to me was ____.

E. SHARING TIME:

Open discussion time about the day's sharing.

F. INTRODUCTION OF REINFORCEMENT ACTIVITY:

The *Sad Sack* is introduced and it is explained that the sharing of sadness will bring about a happier sack. Each day sad thoughts or experiences will be shared. After each sharing, a colorful piece of paper is pasted on the sack. At the end of two days of sharing, everyone will get a reward.

Curricular-Related Activities

A. ART:

Everyone draws a cupboard and puts on the shelves all the things that they didn't have at one time that made them feel sad. The cupboards may be shared with others.

B. DRAMA:

Act out a scene from the *Thought Catcher* by being Mother, dog and cupboard. Share reactions to sad feelings after the scene.

C. GYM (Physical Education):

Someone is chosen to be Mother Hubbard, the dog and the cupboard. The cupboard stands at the end of the room facing away from the group. The Mother and the dog walk to the cupboard. After they are there the Mother asks: "Cupboard, cupboard, do you have a bone for my dog?" The cupboard then decides when to jump around, arms outstretched and yell: "I am empty ! " At that point, the Mother and the dog run back to the goal. The first one there gets to choose three other people to play.

D. FORMING (Language Arts):

The children are asked to write a sad story. The story can be shared. They may share their stories and explain how the characters in their stories are affected by sadness.

Pretending Time

A minimum of 15-20 minutes should be allocated for this activity.

A. READY-SET-GO:

The children get into comfortable positions. Then the facilitator says: "Please relax. . . Enjoy a few moments of quiet. . . Now, I am going to play some quiet music, just relax, listen and enjoy it. . . ." (The music is played for two to three minutes.)

B. PRETENDING:

The facilitator says: "The music has ended and you feel relaxed. . . Quiet is everywhere. . . Now, today I want you to pretend you are a tear drop. . . You live inside someone's tear duct. . . What do you look like? . . . How do you feel? . . . The person is beginning to feel sad. . . You feel a rushing movement. . . And, now, you are being cried out of an eye. . . How do you feel? . . . Now, a soft tissue wipes you away. . . But, before you are wisked off, you see this person smile. . . What do you think happened? How do you feel? . . . ."

C. STOP-LOOK-LISTEN:

The facilitator says: "Inside the soft tissue you are safe. . . Stop pretending. . . You are safe. . . You are warm. . . You are content. And now, your wetness has dried up . . . And you sink into the tissue for a moment. . . Think about what you learned from the pretending and listen carefully to what others learned ! "

D. REFLECTIONS:

The facilitator may ask the following questions:

1. What did you look like being a tear?
2. How did you feel?
3. What did you feel or think as you were cried out of the person's eye?
4. Did you know the person?
5. What happened to make the person happy?
6. Did you mind being wiped away?
7. Was your tear happy or sad or both?
8. What things in your life make tears come falling down on your cheeks?
9. What things or people in your life can make tears stop falling?
10. How do you feel about your tears?

Fable:
"THE MILLER, THE SON AND THE DONKEY"

One day a Miller and his son were driving their donkey to market. They had not gone far when some girls saw them and broke out laughing. "Look!" cried one. "Look at those fools! How silly they are to be trudging along on foot when the donkey might be carrying one of them on its back!"

This seemed to make sense, so the Miller lifted his son on the donkey and walked along contentedly by its side. They trod on for a while until they met an old man who spoke to the son scornfully. "You should be ashamed of yourself, you lazy rascal. What do you mean by riding when your poor old father has to walk? It shows that no one respects age any more. The least you can do is get down and let your father rest his bones."

Red with shame, the son dismounted and made his father get on the donkey's back. They had gone only a little further when they met a group of young fellows who mocked them. "What a cruel old man!" jeered one of the fellows. "There he sits, selfish and comfortable, while the poor boy has to stumble along the dusty road to keep up with him. " So the father lifted the son up and the two of them rode along.

However, before they reached the market place, a townsperson stopped them and said, "Have you no feeling for dumb creatures?" "The way that you load that little animal is a crime. You two men are better able to carry the poor little beast than the beast you!"

Wanting to do the right thing, the Miller and his son got off the donkey, tied its legs together, slung the donkey on a pole and carried it on their shoulders. When the crowd saw this spectacle, the people laughed so loudly that the donkey was frightened, kicked through the cords and, falling off the pole, fell into the river and was drowned.

FOLLOW-UP QUESTIONS:

1. What in this story makes you feel sad?
2. How do you feel when people laugh at you? What do you do with those feelings?
3. Why do you think the Miller and his son were so concerned about what others said to them?
4. What do you do when someone tells you to act in a way other than what you think is right?
5. Do you sometimes laugh at people who behave in a different manner?

Supplemental Activities

SENSE STRETCHERS:

1. Eyes:

The children think of something that they have seen or might see that would cause them to feel sad.

2. Ears:

The children share sounds and words that help make them feel sad or remind them of sad times.

3. Nose:

The children pretend they are a famous detective called "Nosey." Nosey has been assigned to search out all the smells that remind people of sadness. The children can create a list of such smells or even create a story around this idea.

4. Tongue:

The children create an imaginary sad meal. Example might be sad soup made with tears, weepy lettuce, angry asparagus and wailing water.

P. 5. (POST SCRIPT) ACTIVITIES:

1. Poem Pushers:

The children pretend to be the characters in any poem or story that might have sad feelings. These characters then explain who they are and why they are sad. They can also tell what might make them get over their sadness.

2. Song Squeezers:

Favorite songs are sung individually or by small groups in a very sad way with sad actions added if desired.

3. Show Stoppers:

The children may create and present for sale items that are guaranteed to make someone sad.

Session Eight: Sharing Sadness

Rationale

"Sharing sad feelings is a beginning to starting smiles."

K. Morrison

Goals

To identify and claim sad feelings as okay.
To share sad feelings.
To claim some responsibility for sad feelings.

Materials

Tape recorders or note pads and pencils; *Reinforcement Activity: Sad Sack.*

Thought Catcher:
"HUMPTY DUMPTY"

Humpty Dumpty sat on a wall,
Humpty Dumpty had a great fall;
All the king's horses and all the king's men,
Couldn't put Humpty Dumpty together again.

Process Activities

A. DISCUSSION STARTERS:

1. Humpty was probably happy on his wall until he fell, got hurt and no one could put the pieces back together. Have you ever been hurt so badly (feeling-wise or physically) that no one could make you feel better? What was this like? What did you do?
2. Is there someone who usually tries to make you feel better when you feel sad?
3. Is there someone you've tried to help feel better?
4. Are there times when you don't want anyone to put you back together; you just want someone to talk to or to listen to you?

B. REINFORCEMENT ACTIVITY:

The facilitator and the children write something which makes them feel sad on one or more pieces of colored paper. These are shared and pasted on the sack.

C. INTERVIEWING MR. SAD AND MS. TEAR:

Choosing partners, the children (using a tape recorder or paper and pen) interview each other. The children can use prepared questions or make up their own. Some possible questions are:

1. Why are you called Mr. Sad or Ms. Tear?
2. What makes you feel sad?
3. How do you act when you feel sad?
4. Do you like being Ms. Tear or Mr. Sad?
5. Can you ever change your sad feelings?

D. SHARING TIME:

The interviews are shared. What was learned and what was felt during the activities?

E. QUESTION TIME:

The facilitator and the children talk over the following questions:

1. Is it bad to feel sad?
2. Does feeling sad mean you are weak?
3. Boys should not cry. Right?
4. Are girls naturally cry babies?
5. Sharing your sadness with someone is ____________?
6. Responsibility for sad feelings belong to ____________.

Curricular-Related Activities

A. ART:

Hard-boiled eggs or blown eggs are decorated with sad faces and/or thoughts. They can be set on a Humpty Dumpty wall.

B. DRAMA:

The group is divided into two parts. One group stands at the far end of the room in a straight line. The second group chooses a leader and surrounds this leader—all bunch together. When the leader decides, the leader yells "Break !" and all the egg pieces try to reach the opposite goal line before they are tagged by the other group. When all parts of the egg are tagged, the groups change places.

C. GYM (Physical Education):

Act out being Humpty Dumpty, the horses and the soldiers. Check out feelings after the scene is finished.

D. FORMING (Language Arts):

Children are asked to make a get well card for someone they know. The verse should express shared sadness over the accident or illness. Cards can be sent to the person.

Pretending Time

A minimum of 15-20 minutes should be allocated for this activity.

A. READY-SET-GO:

The children are asked to get into comfortable positions. Then the facilitator says: "Please close your eyes. . . Relax. . . This time is for you. . . I will now play some quiet music. . . Just listen and enjoy. . . ."

(Music is played two to three minutes.)

B. PRETENDING:

The facilitator says: "The music is over. . . You are comfortable. Now, I want you to imagine that you have been given the responsibility of handing out the sadness in the world. . . Spend a few moments thinking about this responsibility and how you might do this. . . Now, begin handing out the sadness, as you see fit . . . What is your own reaction to how you handed it out? How do you feel? . . . Did you give any to yourself? . . . "

C. STOP-LOOK-LISTEN:

The facilitator says: "Stop pretending. . . Your job is now over... All the sadness is gone . . . Everything is okay. . . Think back about the pretending; what did you learn? . . . What do you think others learned? . . . Listen. . . ."

REFLECTIONS:

The facilitator may ask the following questions:

1. How did you feel being in charge of handing out the world's sadness?
2. How did you hand it out?
3. To whom did you give the sadness?
4. What was the reaction in others when you gave out sadness?
5. Did you give yourself some?
6. In real life, do you give sadness to others? How? How come?
7. Do other people give you sadness? How? How come?
8. What would you like to do with your sadness if you could do anything you wanted with it?
9. Is your sadness good for you?
10. Are sad feelings okay?

Fable:
"THE ROOSTER AND THE PARTRIDGE"

A man who kept roosters found a tame partridge for sale, bought it and took it home to raise along with the roosters. But the roosters picked on the partridge and chased it off. The partridge was sad because it thought that it was looked down on for being another kind of fowl. After a while, when the man saw the roosters fighting among themselves and not giving up until they had drawn blood from one another, he said to himself, "Well, I won't worry any more about being picked on by them, for I see that they don't even let one another alone."

FOLLOW-UP QUESTIONS:

1. Do you know some people who seem to get picked on a lot? Just yes or no, no names please.
2. Have you ever been picked on?
3. If you have been picked on, how did it feel?
4. Have you ever picked on someone else?
5. Why do you think some people pick on other people?

Supplemental Activities

SENSE STRETCHERS:

1. Eyes:

The children may close their eyes and imagine what sadness might look like using their "mind's eye."

2. Ears:

The children listen to sad music with their eyes closed and then share any feelings or thoughts they experienced. The facilitator can ask them to seek sadness in some way as they listen, or the music can be the only source of direction.

3. Nose:

The children are given small bottles, water, food coloring and some spices. They are asked to individually or in small groups make sad smells—a new perfume to be sold this year. On the label they must write the sad ingredients like loosing a favorite doll, cutting one's knee, or being left out of a party. They may also make up an advertisement to sell such sad stuff.

4. Tongue:

The facilitator brings out a bottle of water which has on it a label saying *Magic Tears.* Each person is poured a small cup of this special water and then sad thoughts are shared.

P. S. (POST SCRIPT) ACTIVITIES:

1. Poem Pushers:

Any poem is read or recited by the children in a very sad voice. Sad body or facial actions will add to the activity.

2. Song Squeezers:

The facilitator and the children choose a favorite melody, add sad words to it and then sing their sad song.

3. Show Stoppers:

The children may create a court scene where sad people are being accused of spreading too much sadness. There can be a judge, two lawyers, the sad person and even a jury. A discussion about the sadness could be conducted.

Evaluation

PERSONAL NOTES

The purpose of the personal notes is to allow and aid reflection. It is important for the facilitator to look back and recapitulate what has occurred thus far and to write down thoughts, feelings and experiences which have happened during the session.

Frequently, progress is difficult to detect while actively engaged in the session. The personal notes will help promote and provide perceivable progress.

Session Nine: Dealing with Sadness

Rationale

"Sadness, like happiness, needs to be shared."

K. Morrison

Goals

To identify, claim and share sad feelings.
To deal with one's own sad feelings and needs.
To deal with other people's sad feelings.

Materials

Role playing cards; board; chalk; *Tear Poster; Reinforcement Activity: Sad Sack; Reinforcement Sticker:* I am responsible for my sad feelings (or material for making them); *Suggested Reward.*

Thought Catcher:
"LITTLE BOY BLUE"

Little Boy Blue, come blow your horn,
The sheep's in the meadow, the cow's in the corn.
Where is the boy that looks after the sheep?
"He's under the haystack, fast asleep."
Will you wake him? "No, not I:
For if I do, he'll be sure to cry."

Process Activities

A. DISCUSSION STARTERS:

1. Can you imagine reasons why Boy Blue would cry?
2. Have you ever stayed away from someone because you knew that person was sad?
3. Are there times when you are sad and want to be left alone?
4. Does not finishing a task make you feel sad?
5. Is is all right to cry?

B. SHARING TIME:

The facilitator writes the following on the board for the children to complete:

When I am sad ______________________________.

I like to be with people who ____________________.

I don't like to be with people who________________.

C. DEALING WITH SADNESS:

The facilitator chooses a child to be Mr. or Ms. Sadness. Then three to four children are chosen to hold cards which contain various replies to sad feelings. Mr/Ms. Sadness thinks of something to share that is sad (made up or real). Mr./Ms. Sadness then shares sad feelings and one by one the card holders read the messages on their cards to Mr./Ms. Sadness. After each card is read, Mr./Ms. Sadness shares feelings that come from the reply. Game players can be changed after each role play.

The cards are made up of helpful and non-helpful messages like the following:

Don't be a cry baby.
Forget it.
It doesn't sound bad to me.
Tell me about it.
Can I help?
I am sorry to hear that.

D. TEAR POSTER:

The facilitator and the children talk about the helpful things to say and do when someone is sad. The *Tear Poster* , may then be put up for display if the children choose.

E. REINFORCEMENT ACTIVITY:

Sad Sack: The facilitator and the children share the little pieces of paper with sad thoughts or experiences and then paste pieces of colored paper on the sack.

F. REINFORCEMENT STICKER:

I am responsible for my sad feelings.

G. SUGGESTED REWARD:

The colorful *Sad Sack* is passed around and each child receives a personal note from the facilitator with an accepting, kind message on it.

Curricular-Related Activities

A. ART:

Draw or paint a picture all in blue, showing all the things that make you sad.

B. DRAMA:

Act out the rhyme, letting the children vocalize as they wish and take action where they want. Check out the feelings at the end of the scene.

C. GYM (Physical Education):

Yellow paper is used as haystacks. There are enough pieces of paper for everyone to stand on except the person chosen to be Boy Blue. Boy Blue stands in the center and pretends to blow a horn. At the blowing of the horn, everyone must find a new haystack—the one left without a haystack becomes the new Boy Blue.

D. FORMING (Language Arts):

The children are asked to make a list of reasons why Boy Blue cried and what might make him feel better. The paper could be set up as follows:

BOY BLUE

WHY CRIES	POSSIBLE SOLUTION
1.____________________	1.____________________
2.____________________	2.____________________

Pretending Time

A minimum of 15-20 minutes should be allocated for this activity.

A. READY-SET-GO:

The children get into comfortable positions. Then the facilitator says: "Please close your eyes. . . Enjoy some quiet music I will play for you. . . Just relax and listen. . . ."

(Music is played two or three minutes.)

B. PRETENDING:

The facilitator says: "The music has stopped, but you just keep enjoying the quiet. . . Now, I want you to begin hearing a soft, faint faraway crying sound. . . The sound is now coming closer... The crying is getting louder . . . Whoever is crying is now behind you, turn around. . . Who is it? . . . Why is that person crying? . . . What do you do? . . . What do you say? . . . What does this person do? . . . Now, spend some time with this person, doing what you want. . . The crying has ended. . . The person leaves. . . How do you feel? . . ."

C. STOP-LOOK-LISTEN:

The facilitator says: "It is quiet again. . . Stop pretending. . . There is no crying. . . It is just quiet and peaceful. . . Now, take some time to think about the pretending. . . Look at what you have learned. . . Listen to what others have learned. . . ."

D. REFLECTIONS:

The facilitator may ask the following questions:

1. What were your thoughts when you heard the crying?
2. As the crying got closer, what did you want to do or say?
3. Who was crying when you turned around?
4. What did you do?
5. What did you say?
6. Why did the person stop crying?
7. How did you feel when the person stopped crying?
8. What makes you cry in real life?
9. What can others do for you when you are crying?
10. Is crying a normal thing that everyone does?

Fable:
"THE FISHERMEN WHO CAUGHT A STONE"

Some fishermen were hauling on their net, which was so big and heavy that they began to dance for joy, thinking that they had a big catch. When they pulled it out onto the shore, they found that they had very few fish and a net full of stones and wood. They were quite dejected, not so much out of disappointment at what had happened, but because they had anticipated the opposite. One of them, an old man, said, "Enough of this, my friends. Grief is apparently the sister of joy. Since we had so much fun in anticipation, we must also have some grief."

FOLLOW-UP QUESTIONS:

1. When was the last time you were disappointed? When you thought a good thing was going to happen but didn't?
2. Do you expect something is going to hapen even though you really don't have reasons to think so?
3. How do you usually act when you are disappointed?
4. When was the last time you disappointed someone?
5. How would be the best way to act if one gets disappointed?

Supplemental Activities

SENSE STRETCHERS:

1. Eyes:

The children are all given a paper bag on which they draw a sad face. The bags are then filled with real or imaginary objects that make the individual feel sad.

2. Ears:

The children (individually or in small groups) create and share sad stories. Happy endings may be added.

3. Nose:

The children close their eyes and to try and imagine what sadness smells like. This is then shared with the group.

4. Tongue:

Sad sandwiches are made from bread, peanut butter, jam and honey. Then sad faces are put on the top piece of bread with cake frosting, nuts, raisins and so forth. The sad sandwich is then eaten and the imaginary results of eating sadness is shared.

P. S. (POST SCRIPT) ACTIVITIES:

1. Poem Pushers:

The children choose or are assigned a sad character from a poem (*Humpty Dumpty*, the dog in *Old Mother Hubbard, Old Mother Hubbard* and so forth. The characters then get together and try to decide who has the most reason to be sad.

2. Song Squeezers:

The children are divided into three groups. The groups will then be asked to sing every song in sad, happy or angry voices. One song is chosen and the facilitator points to the group to sing and then changes the groups at will with the song changing from one feeling to another.

3. Show Stoppers:

The children can act out a melodrama where there is an angry person, a sad person and a hero who brings happiness. Clapping and booing are accepted.

Evaluation

1. What I liked *best* about the Sad Feelings Sessions was ____________________

2. What I liked *least* about the Sad Feelings Sessions was ____________________

3. What I wanted to happen in these Sad Feelings Sessions which *never* came about was ____________________

   ____

4. During the Sad Feelings Sessions, I wish I would have — ____________________

5. My overall *feelings* about the Sad Feelings Sessions are ____________________

unit four

unkind feelings

Learning to deal with personal hurt is a difficult task, but hurt occurs and learning to understand it is necessary. One must come to grow even from unkind experiences. The following sessions focus upon unkind actions. These experiences help one understand that unkindness exists, but that positive growth can be a result.

The materials needed for the next three sessions, including the *Reinforcement Activity, Suggested Reward* and *Reinforcement Sticker* are presented here for your preparation.

SESSION TEN: FEELING UNKIND

Ties made of cloth, ribbon or yarn; paper sacks; newspapers; large garbage can, *Reinforcement Activity: Treasure Hunt.*

Treasure Hunt

A large piece of construction paper, tag board or cloth can be used for the background of this activity. Feet (equal to the number of participants, doubled,) can be made of various materials (paper, cloth, tag bard) and placed in an up and down manner over clues that lead to the treasure hunt chest. As each person shares a sad feeling in sessions eleven and twelve a foot is removed and the clue exposed. The description of the treasure is written under the treasure chest and not revealed until the last foot is removed.

SESSION ELEVEN: CHALLENGING THE UNKIND MONSTER

Paper; magazines; bits and pieces; glue; crayons; scissors; *Reinforcement Activity: Treasure Hunt.*

SESSION TWELVE: BECOMING GUARDIANS OF UNKINDNESS

Twenty to thirty objects (stones, nails, cotton, sandpaper. lace, dirt), *Unkind Mask, Reinforcement Activity: Treasure Hunt; Suggested Reward:* Golden Popcorn or Silver Hershey Kisses; and *Reinforcement Sticker:* I am responsible for my unkind feelings (or material to make them).

Session Ten: Feeling Unkind

Rationale

"How do I know what I think until I feel what I do?"

J. Bruner

Goals

To identify and experience unkindness in self and others.

Materials

Ties made of cloth, ribbon or yarn. ; paper sacks; newspapers; large garbage can; *Reinforcement Activity: Treasure Hunt.*

Thought Catcher:
"DING DONG BELL"

Ding dong, bell,
Pussy's in the well!
Who put her in?
Little Tommy Lin.
Who pulled her out?
Big Johnny Stout.
What a naughty boy was that
To try to drown poor pussy cat.
Who never did him any harm,
But killed the mice in his father's barn.

Process Activities

A. DISCUSSION STARTERS:

1. Can you imagine the feelings and thoughts that Tommy Lin, Johnny Stout and the pussy cat might have in this rhyme?
2. Do you ever feel like really hurting someone or something? Explain.
3. What have you done when you saw unkindness being done to someone or something?
4. Do you feel differently about someone or something being harmed when that person or thing never harms others?
5. Do you think you usually behave more like Johnny Stout than you do like Tommy Lin? How do you feel about your response to this question?

B. UNKIND ANIMAL ACTIVITY:

The facilitator explains that the activity they are about to do has one ground rule: ***No physical hurting.*** Then the children are asked to find a partner and one person in each group is given a tie to wear. Then the children decide what animal they want to be.

The facilitator then instructs the children to play nicely with their partner. After a few minutes, the facilitator tells the individuals wearing ties to do or say something unkind to their partner and the partner is asked to react verbally. The activity is repeated after ties are exchanged.

C. QUESTION TIME:

1. How did you feel when you and your partner were playing nicely?
2. How did you feel when your partner was unkind to you?
3. What did you feel like doing when your partner was unkind?
4. What did it feel like when you decided to be unkind?

D. UNKIND BAGS:

Everyone is given a large paper bag and some old newspapers. Individuals then find a place by themselves (a large room is best for this activity). The papers are then crumbled as each person thinks of unkindnesses done by self or others. The crumbled papers are placed in the large bags. After the bags are filled, the bags can be hit, stepped on and thrown into the garbage can.

E. SHARING TIME:

Open sharing time about feelings of unkindness— what they do to us and to others.

F. INTRODUCTION OF REINFORCEMENT ACTIVITY:

Treasure Hunt. Little feet, which when raised after sharing unkind feelings give clues to the treasure, are placed on a large piece of paper. The treasure is also made so it can be opened at the end of the game and the treasure is written there. (The number of feet can be two times the number of participants so each person can have a chance to share each day.)

Curricular-Related Activities

A. ART:

Everyone is asked to draw or design a warning bell. The children decorate and write on their own bells warnings of unkindness that they have experienced or want others to be aware of. An area in the room where all the bells could then be hung up is suggested.

B. DRAMA:

Once again, act out parts of "Ding Dong Bell," allowing the children freedom of words and actions. Check the children's feelings after the scene ends.

C. GYM (Physical Education):

A circle is formed with everyone holding hands at arms length apart. Someone is chosen to be the cat and is put in the center of the circle. Then someone is chosen to be Johnny Stout. Johnny then tries to get in to rescue the cat. The children can move hands up and down to help the cat out. After five tries, if Johnny hasn't rescued the cat by getting inside the circle, that person becomes the cat and a new Johnny is picked by the old cat. If Johnny rescues the cat, both players get to choose new people for the next game.

D. FORMING (Language Arts):

The children are asked to write (individually or with a partner) a radio news report of the *Pussy Cat in the Well* incident. A pretend mike can be used when the various news reports are read. (This may lead to a discussion about accountability of news reporting.)

Pretending Time

A minimum of 15-20 minutes should be allocated for this activity.

A. READY-SET-GO:

The children get into comfortable positions. Then the facilitator says: "Please let yourself relax. . . Let yourself enjoy doing nothing. . . It is easy. . . Now, I want you to imagine soft falling snow. . . Big beautiful flakes are gently falling all around you, but you are warm. . . Watch them slowly fall. . . Big beautiful snow flakes falling... Falling...."

B. PRETENDING:

The facilitator says: "Now, let the snow flakes slowly stop falling. There is no more snow . . . Just quiet air. . . Now, I want you to pretend you are a 'Streak of Meanness'. . . What do you look like? . . . How do you feel? . . . What do you want to do? . . . Now, I want you to see two children coming toward you. . . As they come closer, they know that you are a 'Streak of Meanness'. . . Your meanness is slowing fading away and you are becoming yourself ...."

C. STOP-LOOK-LISTEN:

The facilitator says: "Stop pretending. . . You are left alone with your meanness. . . What does it feel like? . . . Now, slowly your meanness is fading away. . . It is disappearing. . . It is almost gone. . . Now, you are left feeling calm and quiet. . . It feels good. Enjoy this calm and quiet for a few moments . . . And now, when you are ready, look back at the pretending. . . What do you think you learned? . . . What do you think others learned? ... Listen."

D. REFLECTIONS:

The facilitator may ask the following questions:

1. What did you look like as a "Streak of Meanness?"
2. What feelings did you have as the "Streak of Meanness?"
3. What thoughts did you have as the "Streak of Meanness?"
4. What did the children do when they saw you?
5. Did you know the children?
6. What did you do or say to the children?
7. What was it like being left alone feeling mean?
8. Were you glad or sad when the meanness began to disappear?
9. In real life, can you remember a time when you walked around like a "Streak of Meanness?"
10. How do people react to you when you are mean?
11. How do you feel when someone is mean to you?
12. What do you wish people would do with their mean feelings?

Fable:
"THE FOX AND THE CROW"

A crow had stolen a good sized piece of cheese from a cottage window and had flown with it into a tall tree. A fox who had seen this happen, said, "If I am smart, I will have cheese for supper tonight." The fox thought for a moment and then decided on a plan.

"Good afternoon, crow," the fox said. "How really beautiful you look today. I've never seen your feathers so glistening. Your neck is as graceful as a swan's and your wings are mightier than an eagle's. I am sure that if you had a voice, you would sing as sweetly as a nightengale."

The crow, pleased with such praise, wanted to prove that it could sing. As soon as it opened its mouth to caw, the cheese fell to the ground and the fox snapped it up.

As the fox trotted off, to make it worse by calling back to the crow, "I may have talked much about your beauty, but I said nothing about your brains."

FOLLOW-UP QUESTIONS:

1. Please share how you feel about the actions of the Fox and the Crow.
2. Has someone ever tricked you into doing something and gotten you into trouble or gotten you hurt? How do you feel about such things?
3. Can you think of things that look or sound great but really hurt people?
4. Have you ever over-praised or flattered someone so that person would like you?
5. Is it ever okay to trick a person to get that person to do what you wish?

Supplemental Activities

SENSE STRETCHERS:

1. Eyes:

The children are asked to share unkind things they have seen in their lifetime.

2. Ears:

Unkind words or sounds that the children have heard or used themselves are shared.

3. Nose:

"Nosey," the detective, is scared of unkind sounds. The children can list such unkind sounds or create a story for Nosey.

4. Tongue:

The children list all the unkind things this *Unkind Tongue* has said and they are written down on the board. Then individual children come up and tell *Unkind Tongue* a word or words to use in place of a word on the board. Then the word on the board is erased. A time limit can be set and it can become a race of kindness v.s. unkindness.

P. S. (POST SCRIPT) ACTIVITIES:

1. Poem Pushers:

The children are asked to read or recite poems in an angry, unkind, sad or happy manner while individuals or the class guesses which feeling thev are expressing and showing.

2. Song Squeezers:

The children can sing and act out favorite songs in an unkind way.

3. Show Stoppers:

The facilitator has unkind words on a series of cards. The cards are handed out. The children then create a scene using those words. This can be done either individually or in small groups.

Evaluation

SELF-EVALUATION PROGRESS CHECK

	Extremely	*Very*	*Reasonably*	*Slightly*	*Not at All*
1. How comfortable was I during the session?					
2. Were the children comfortable during the session?					
3. Were the children willing to share feelings freely?					
4. How well did the children accept the feelings of others?					
5. How accepting was I of the children's responses?					
6. How eager were the children to participate?					
7. How well did the children listen?					
8. Was the environment supportive and safe?					
9. How effective were the questions that I asked?					
10. How interested did the group appear to be?					

Session Eleven: Challenging the Unkind Monster

Rationale

"Unkindness, like kindness, can be contagious."

K. Morrison

Goals

To identify and accept responsibility for unkind feelings.
To share unkind feelings.

Materials

Paper; magazines; bits and pieces; glue; crayons; scissors; *Reinforcement Activity: Treasure Hunt.*

Thought Catcher:
"THE QUEEN OF HEARTS"

The Queen of Hearts,
She made some tarts,
All on a summer's day.
The Knave of Hearts,
He stole the tarts,
And took them clean away.

The King of Hearts
Called for the tarts,
And beat the Knave full sore;
The Knave of Hearts
Brought back the tarts,
And vowed he'd steal no more.

Process Activities

A. DISCUSSION STARTERS:

1. Can you image why the Knave stole the tarts?
2. Have you ever done something, then gotten caught, punished and swore you would never do it again?
3. Does fear of being caught and punished keep you from doing unkind things?
4. Would you have told on the Knave?
5. Is it ever all right to tell on someone?

B. UNKIND FANTASY AND RE-RUN:

The facilitator asks the children to get comfortable and relaxed. Then they are asked to remember a time when they were unkind. Then they are instructed to just relax and think of something else for a minute or two. (The facilitator can structure this part by asking them to imagine a specific thing like blue sky, yellow flowers and so forth.)

Then the children are asked to re-run the unkind scene they had a few minutes earlier, but this time to make a different choice of behavior.

C. QUESTION TIME:

1. What happened in your first fantasy?
2. What unkind thing did you do? How did it feel?
3. In the second fantasy, how did you change your behavior? How did that feel?

D. UNKIND MONSTERS:

The facilitator and the children create an *Unkind Monster* from paper, magazines and bits and pieces. The *Unkind Monster* should represent how each person pictures the unkindness of self and others.

E. SHARING TIME:

The facilitator and the children share their *Unkind Monsters*; why they made them like they did based on how they see unkindness in self and others.

F. REINFORCEMENT ACTIVITY:

Treasure Hunt. The facilitator and the children share an unkindness in their lives and lift up clue feet (see page 118).

Curricular-Related Activities

A. ART:

The children make various colorful and decorative hearts, but each one is then cut in two. These broken hearts are placed under a sign that reads: "UNKIND DEEDS BREAK HEARTS."

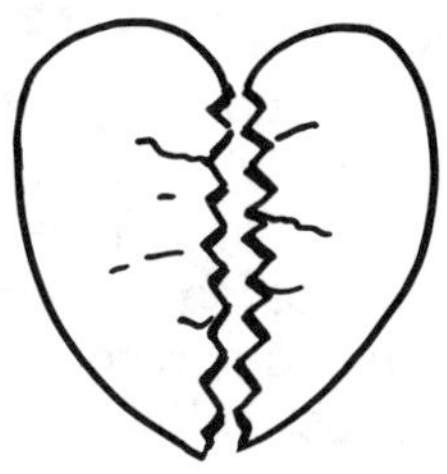

B. DRAMA:

The children act out the parts of Queen, King, Knave and tarts. All share feelings after the scene is completed and a discussion of the relationship of unkindness to individuals could follow.

C. GYM (Physical Education):

Relay Race: Three to four items (paper, cotton balls, sticks and so forth) are placed on several plates. The first person runs down, picks up an object and returns it to another plate. When all of the objects are picked up, the second person takes one and returns it to the first plate. The race continues until one group finishes first.

D. FORMING (Language Arts):

The children are asked to write a newspaper report of the *Queen of Hearts* incident. This is typed up and they are all displayed to see the variety of reports and the different emphases. A discussion about newspaper reporting could follow this writing activity.

Pretending Time

A minimum of 15-20 minutes should be allocated for this activity.

A. READY-SET-GO:

The children get into comfortable positions. Then the facilitator says: "Please let yourself do nothing. . . Just relax. . . It is easy... Now, I want you to imagine it is a beautiful, sunny fall day and you are lying under a big leafy tree. . . You feel a soft, warm breeze blow across your body. . . As the breeze softly blows, the leaves of many colors slowly fall through the air. . . Take a few moments now to enjoy the falling leaves. . . They fall quietly. . . You rest quietly. . . It is a beautiful time. . . ."

B. PRETENDING:

The facilitator says: "Today, I want you to become the 'Streak of Meanness' again. . . What do you look like? . . . How do you feel? . . . What do you want to do? . . . Now, I want you to see someone coming toward you. . . How do you feel about this person? . . . What do you do? . . . The person smiles at you. . . What do you do? . . . The person gently touches you. . . What do you do? . . . How do you feel? . . . The person says: 'I want to help you, please come home with me.' . . . What do you do? . . . How do you feel? . . . The person starts home. . . What do you do? . . . Now, slowly let go of being the 'Streak of Meanness' and become yourself. . . ."

C. STOP-LOOK-LISTEN:

The facilitator says: "Stop pretending. . . The person is now gone and you are alone. . . You are feeling tired. . . Tired of being mean. . . So you let all the meanness you feel slip away. . . Let it go. . . Let it leave you completely. . . You are now quiet. . . Think about the pretending. . . What was it like?. . . What did you learn? . . . Listen to what others thought and felt. . . ."

D. REFLECTIONS:

The facilitator may ask the following questions:

1. Were you the same 'Streak of Meanness' as last time or different?
2. How did it feel to be mean?
3. Who was the person who came toward you?
4. How did you feel about this person?
5. When the person smiled, what did you do?
6. When the person touched you, what did you do?
7. When the person asked you to come home, what did you do?
8. In real life, do you like to be treated kindly when you feel mean?

Fable:
"THE KID ON THE HOUSETOP AND THE WOLF"

A kid stood on a housetop and made nasty remarks to a wolf who was passing by. The wolf said to the kid, "It's not you who are making nasty remarks; it's your position."

FOLLOW-UP QUESTIONS:

1. What do you think was the meaning of what the wolf said to the kid?
2. How come the kid made remarks to the wolf while standing on the housetop?
3. Do you sometimes feel more brave when you are closer to home?
4. Where is a safe place for you?
5. If you were standing in a safe place, whom might you make remarks to if that person were passing by?

Supplemental Activities

SENSE STRETCHERS:

1. Eyes:

The children are asked to create an unkind face individually or in small groups.

This can be painted, drawn or made out of construction paper. The unkind faces are then shared. If they are made mask size, they can be used for the following ear *Sense Stretcher.*

2. Ears:

The children make unkind faces or stand behind the unkind masks made earlier and share unkind words they have heard. After each sharing, the children share how they felt hearing those words.

3. Nose:

The children are asked to bring in or verbally create a mixture of things that might create an unkind smell to someone's nose. Examples might be tobasco sauce and chili pepper, strong soap or an old piece of fruit.

P. S. (POST SCRIPT) ACTIVITIES:

Some suggested *P.S. Activities* for this session are:

1. Poem Pushers:

The children decide as a group what should be the consequences for the unkind people in various poems like *Ding Dong Bell, The Queen of Hearts, I Had a Little Pony* and any others.

2. Song Squeezers:

A favorite song is chosen and then groups of children compete to sing it in the most unkind way. The winning team gets to choose the next song.

3. Show Stoppers:

The children act out a feeling of unkindness, happiness, sadness or anger and the child to guess the feeling gets the next turn to act out a feeling.

Evaluation

PERSONAL NOTES

The purpose of the personal notes is to allow and aid reflection. It is important for the facilitator to look back and recapitulate what has occurred thus far and to write down thoughts, feelings and experiences which have happened during the session.

Frequently, progress is difficult to detect while actively engaged in the session. The personal notes will help promote and provide perceivable progress.

Session Twelve: Becoming Guardians of Unkindness

Rationale

"The decision to be unkind is always a personal choice."

K. Morrison

Goals

To identify and accept responsibility for unkind feelings.
To share unkind feelings in a responsible way.

Materials

Twenty to thirty objects (stones, nails, cotton, sandpaper, lace, dirt), *Unkind Mask, Reinforcement Activity: Treasure Hunt; Suggested Reward*: Golden Popcorn or Silver Hershey Kisses; and *Reinforcement Sticker:* I am responsible for my unkind feelings (or material to make them.)

Thought Catcher:
"I HAD A LITTLE PONY"

**I had a little pony,
His name was Dapplegray;
I lent him to a lady,
To ride a mile away.**

**She whipped him, she slashed him,
She rode him through the mire;
I would not lend my pony now,
For all the lady's hire.**

Process Activities

A. DISCUSSION STARTERS:

1. If the lady had been unkind to your pony, what would you have done?

2. Is it hard to tell older people you don't like things they do or say? (Principal, teacher, parents, relatives, doctor and so forth.)

3. Has anyone ever been unkind to something of yours? What did you feel and do?

4. How about you, do you ever treat people or animals in an unkind manner?

5. Do you think some people are more sensitive to the feelings of people and animals than are other people? If so, how come? If not, why not?

B. UNKIND OBJECT ACTIVITY:

The facilitator and the children look over the objects and, in their minds, choose one or two that remind them how they feel when unkind. When everyone has mentally chosen an object, it is shared with others by picking it up and telling why that object reminds them of their unkindness. If time allows, the activity can be repeated by choosing an object based on how a person feels when others are unkind.

C. UNKIND SACK ACTIVITY:

Everyone takes turns placing the *Unkind Sack* (a paper bag with an unkind mask) over their heads and saying: "I am unkind when I ______________________." The sack is removed and the person says: "I can change that unkindness by ______________________." This activity can be repeated, depending on the willingness of the participants.

Curricular-Related Activities

A. ART:

A large pony is drawn on an area of the room. Children, during their free time, can come up and write in an unkindness done to them and color, chalk, or paint in the area. The end result will be a patchwork pony of many colors.

B. DRAMA:

Act out a short play concerning the "Lady", "Pony" and "Boy" and then discuss feelings and thoughts. This activity can provide sight and learning.

C. GYM (Physical Education):

Someone is chosen to be the "Boy" and stands at the end of the room beside an object that is home (goal). All the other children line up at the other end of the room. Then the first two children stand on a place named "Lady" and "Pony." When ready, the "Boy" yells: "Run, Pony, Run ! " and both the "Lady" and the "Pony" run to the home plate. The first one there gets to be the "Boy". The game is repeated.

D. FORMING (Language Arts):

The children are asked to write a series of interview questions to ask the owner of the pony and the lady who whipped the pony on a television talk show. Then the questions are used in a pretend television show.

Pretending Time

A minimum of 15-20 minutes should be allocated for this activity.

A. READY-SET-GO:

The children assume comfortable positions. Then the facilitator says: "Please relax. . . Take a few moments to rest. . . Let yourself enjoy doing nothing. . . It is easy. . . Now, I want you to imagine a beautiful field of flowers. . . It is a wonderful field of flowers that slowly and softly move as a breeze gently blows through them. . . Lie down in this field. . . Become a part of this beautiful scene. . . Smell the flowers. . . Hear the gentle moving of the flowers around you. . . Feel the soft warm breeze. . . Just enjoy being a part of the lovely scene...."

B. PRETENDING:

The facilitator says: "You are relaxed and at home in this field. . . Now, I want you to slowly sit up . . . At the end of the field is a dark curtain. . . I want you to walk toward that curtain. . . Behind that curtain you will find some of your unkindness. . . Hiding behind this curtain is something unkind you did. . . Now, slowly touch the curtain. . . And now, very carefully you can slowly open it. . . What did you see? . . . How do you feel? . . . Take this unkindness and go and show it to someone. . . Whom did you show it to? . . . What did they do? . . . How did you feel? . . . Take this unkindness now and put it somewhere where you want it to stay. . . Now, leave the unkindness and come back to the field. . . Lie down among the flowers. . . How do you feel? . . ."

C. STOP-LOOK-LISTEN:

The facilitator says: "Stop pretending. . . The unkindness is gone. . . Be very quiet. . . Now, when you are ready, look back on the pretending. . . What did you learn? . . . What did others learn? . . . Listen."

D. REFLECTIONS:

The facilitator may ask the following questions:

1. Describe how you felt in the field of flowers?
2. What did you feel when you saw the dark curtain?
3. What was behind the curtain?
4. To whom did you show this unkindness?
5. What did this person do or say?
6. How did you feel about showing it?
7. Where did you finally put this unkindness?
8. How did you feel once this unkindness was gone?
9. In real life, how do you show unkindness to people?
10. When someone is unkind to you, what do you want to do or say to them?

Fable:
"THE FOX AND GOAT IN THE WELL"

A fox fell into a well and had to stay there without any prospect of getting out. A thirsty goat came to the well and, when the goat saw the fox, asked the fox if the water was good. The fox was delighted with this opportunity, sang the praises of the water at great length, told how good it was and invited the goat to come on down.

The goat jumped in without stopping to think it over because it had its mind on nothing but thirst. As soon as the goat's thirst was quenched, it began to reflect along with the fox about how to get out. The fox had a good idea how to save them both. "If you will brace your forefeet, I can climb on your back and jump out." So, the fox climbed on the goat's back, jumped out and ran away.

FOLLOW-UP QUESTIONS:

1. Have you ever heard the old saying: "Look before you leap?" What do you think it means?
2. Have you ever done something without thinking about it and then been sorry?
3. Is it often not so bad if someone else is in the same difficulty in which you are?
4. Have you ever tried to trick someone into helping you?
5. Have you ever wanted something so badly that you would have been easily tricked into doing something without thinking?

Supplemental Activities

SENSE STRETCHERS:

1. Eyes:

The facilitator can have a large circle drawn to represent the world on paper or on the board. The children then list all the things that would go into an unkind world. If there is time, possible solutions for getting rid of specific unkindnesses can also be suggested by the children.

2. Ears:

A *Kind King* and *Kind Queen* are chosen to sit on a pretend throne. Unkind cases are brought before them to hear and they must help the person to find a new way—a kinder way— to express unkind feelings. Children can make up their own unkind cases to present or can be assigned cases by the facilitator.

3. Nose:

The facilitator has a jar and several strong smelling cooking spices, herbs and sauces. As a child shares an unkind experience, real or pretend, some ingredients are added to the jar. After an awful mixture has been created, the unkindness can be passed around for a smell.

P. S. (POST SCRIPT) ACTIVITIES:

1. Poem Pushers:

The children take the role of the parents of an unkind poem—characters like Tommy Lin, the Knave and the Lady in *I Had a Little Pony* plus any others. The parents of these characters then explain how they feel about what their children have done.

2. Song Squeezers:

Songs are sung by individuals or small groups in an unkind, angry, sad or happy manner. The same song can be sung with the feelings expressed chosen by the facilitator.

3. Show Stoppers:

A melodrama can again be created with characters who show feelings of happiness, sadness, unkindness and anger. Children can boo and clap and hiss as the scene is performed.

Evaluation

1. What I liked *best* about the Unkind Feelings Sessions was ____________________
2. What I liked *least* about the Unkind Feelings Sessions was ____________________
3. What I wanted to happen in these Unkind Feeling Sessions which *never* came about was ____________________

   ____
4. During the Unkind Feelings Sessions, I wish I would have ____________________
5. My overall *feelings* about the Unkind Feelings Sessions are ____________________

unit five

fear feelings

Even if one has a very positive self-image, fear is a very real feeling. However, there is a distinct difference between rational and irrational fear ! The next sessions are to help children realize that it is all right to be afraid and that fear can often provide good guidlines for safety. But, too much fear or fear that has no basis can be harmful. However rational fear can be an enabling act and aid the development of positive self-image.

The materials needed for the next three sessions are presented here for your preparation.

SESSION THIRTEEN: COVERING UP FEAR

Large piece of paper; various colored paper; scissors; glue; marking pens; another large piece of paper or a blackboard; *Reinforcement Activity: Door of Fear.* Each child and the facilitator make their own black doors with white space on which to write or paste on pieces of paper. The children can verbally share things they fear if they want.

SESSION FOURTEEN: FREEING FEAR

Dough ready for shaping and baking (frozen commercial dough in small containers), *Fear Face*; small pieces of paper; jam or butter; brown paper or tin foil; oven; pans; hot pads; napkins: *Reinforcement Activity: Door of Fear.*

Fear Face. A *Fear Face* is made of paper and placed over a bag or box. The mouth is cut out; it must be big enough for small pieces of paper to be put in. (For younger children who cannot write, just the face is made.)

SESSION FIFTEEN: FEAR: BAD GUY—GOOD GUY FEELINGS

Good Guy Hat; Bad Guy Hat; Fear Cards; Reinforcement Activity: Door of Fear; Suggested Reward and *Reinforcement Sticker*: I am responsible for my feelings of fear.

Hats. Hats can be made out of paper or be real hats with signs on them; bags with faces and so forth.

Suggested Reward. The reward is individually arranged between facilitator and child.

Reinforcement Sticker: I am responsible for my feelings of fear.

Session Thirteen: Covering Up Fear

Rationale

"When I hide my emotions my stomach keeps score."

Merrill Harmin and Saville Sax

Goals

To identify fear sources.
To share fear feelings.

Materials

Large piece of paper; various colored paper; scissors; glue; marking pens; another large piece of paper or a blackboard; *Reinforcement Activity: Door of Fear.*

Thought Catcher:
"LITTLE MISS MUFFET"

Little Miss Muffet
Sat on a tuffet,
Eating her curds and whey,
Along came a big spider,
That sat down beside her
And frightened Miss Muffet away!

Process Activities

A. DISCUSSION STARTERS:

1. What was there about the spider that might have made Miss Muffet scared?
2. What things or people scare you?
3. How do you think the spider felt?
4. When you are scared what do you do?
5. Are you sometimes scared but pretend or act as if you aren't? If you do, how come?

B. CRAZY FEAR QUILT:

A large piece of paper is placed in an open accessible place. Many various colored papers and materials, such as ribbon, rickrack or tape are made available. Then the facilitator and the children select from such materials items on which they write (in black pens) things people fear. These are then pasted on the large paper and the quilt is hung up over the blackboard or another large piece of paper.

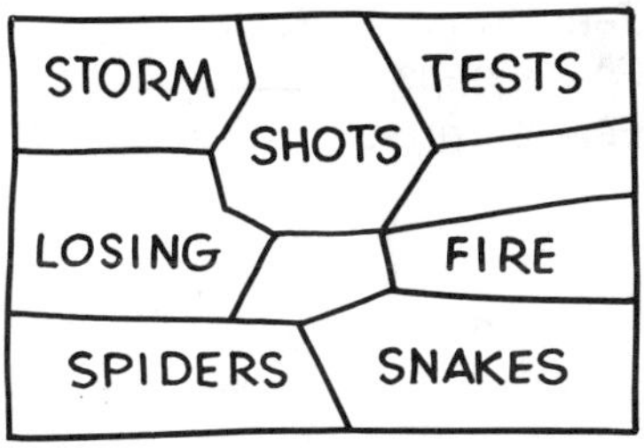

C. SHARING TIME:

Together, the facilitator and the children share all the things which make up the *Crazy Fear Quilt.*

Next, the facilitator asks the children to think of something they fear that they may find difficult sharing. Then one by one, individuals go up to the *Crazy Fear Quilt* and, in private, write their fear behind it on the board or paper provided. (Younger children can draw pictures or stand behind the quilt and verbalize the fear.)

E. UNCOVERING FEAR ACTIVITY:

The *Crazy Fear Quilt* is removed and together the children and the facilitator share the feelings and thoughts about their fears.

F. MORE SHARING TIME:

The facilitator asks the children to complete the following open-ended statements:

Fear says________________.
Fear eats________________.
Fear hides_______________.
Fear loves _____________.
Fear drinks_____________.
Fear sleeps_____________.
Fear surprises______.

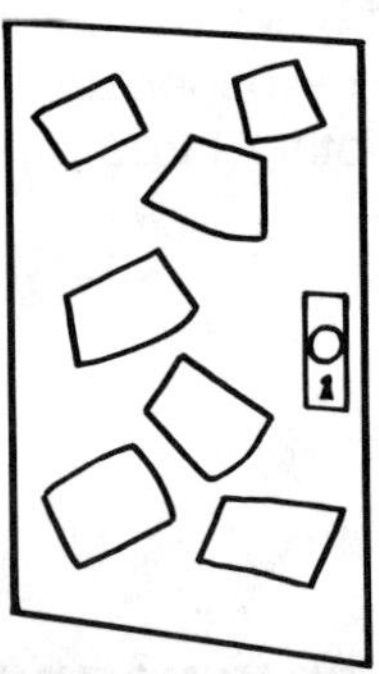

G. INTRODUCTION OF REINFORCEMENT ACTIVITY:

Door of Fear: The facilitator gives each person a black piece of paper made to look like a door with white spaces for writing on. It is then explained that each day people are being asked to write one or more fear on their door and share it with the rest of the group if they wish. Prearranged individual rewards will be given.

Curricular-Related Activities

A. ART:

The making of scary things real and unreal can be done with various media and displayed. A discussion about fears of real and unreal things could follow.

B. DRAMA:

Act out parts, even the tuffet, and share feelings and thoughts at the completion of the scene.

C. GYM (Physical Education):

Someone is Miss Muffet. That person sits, with back to the group, on a cushion. A child is chosen to be the spider, who sneaks up on Miss Muffet and touches the person softly on the head. At this point, Miss Muffet chases the spider back to the goal. If Miss Muffet catches the spider, she is given another turn. If the spider gets back untagged, then the spider becomes Miss Muffet. With a large group, there can be several Miss Muffets and spiders—with the facilitator giving a vocal signal for running back home.

D. FORMING (Language Arts):

The facilitator plays music that creates possible fearful sounds. The children shut their eyes and imagine fearful colors and moving shapes. This is followed by the children writing a description of their feelings and the various colors and shapes that come to them.

Pretending Time

A minimum of 15-20 minutes should be allocated for this activity.

A. READY-SET-GO:

The children get into comfortable positions. Then the facilitator says: "Please let yourself become quiet. . . Just relax. . . Now, I want you to become aware of your feet. . . Let them relax. . . Now, become aware of your lower legs. . . Let them relax. . . Now, upper legs. . . Relax. . . Now, your upper body. . . Relax. . . Now, become aware of your head. . . Just let it relax. . . Your whole body is now relaxed. . . Just take a few moments to enjoy this."

B. PRETENDING:

The facilitator says: "Today, I want you to image yourself in a beautiful woods. . . Now, take a few moments to enjoy yourself... Everything is peaceful and beautiful . . . But, suddenly, you are aware of something else. . . It is coming closer. . . You begin to feel afraid. . . What do you want to do? . . . Now, look closely through the woods and see what has been scaring you. . . What is it? . . . What do you do? . . . The scary thing now goes back into the woods. . . Everything is peaceful and beautiful again."

C. STOP-LOOK-LISTEN:

The facilitator says: "Take a few moments to enjoy the woods again. . . Stop pretending, you are no longer afraid. . . You feel very safe. . . Now, think about the pretending. . . What did you learn? . . . What do you think others learned? . . . Listen. . . ."

D. REFLECTIONS:

The facilitator may ask the following questions:

1. Describe how you felt being in that beautiful woods.
2. What were your feelings when you became aware of something else?
3. As this thing came closer and closer, what did you think and feel?
4. What was the scary thing you finally saw?
5. What did you do?
6. When the scary thing went back into the woods, how did you feel?
7. What things really scare you in real life?
8. What do you do when you feel scared?
9. Have you ever scared some one on purpose?
10. Have you ever been scared on purpose? How did you feel about it?

Fable:
"THE GREAT AND LITTLE FISHES"

"We are the terrors of the deep," said the great fishes. "Everything is afraid of us; we fear nothing. You, little fishes, do not count. You cannot fight; you are easily captured."

At that moment, a fisherman lowered a strong, new net. The great fishes were quickly caught and hauled into the ship while the little fishes escaped through the wide meshes.

FOLLOW-UP QUESTIONS:

1. What are your feelings toward the Little Fishes? The Great Fishes?
2. Did your feelings change after the Great Fishes got caught?
3. What big things scare you?
4. Are all big things scary?
5. Are there some advantages about being small? How about being big?
6. Do bigger people sometimes try to push smaller people around? If you think that they do, why do you think they do that?

Supplemental Activities

SENSE STRETCHERS:

Some suggested *Sense Stretchers* that might be used in this session are:

1. Eyes:

The children are asked to share pictures or memories of scary things they have seen.

2. Ears:

Scary sounds can be shared by children. These sounds can be demonstrated or discussed.

3. Nose:

The children share the smells they associate with scary places, things or people.

4. Tongue:

The children think of share words that might cause them to feel afraid. Then a flavor is chosen for each word.

P. S. (POST SCRIPT) ACTIVITIES:

Some suggested *P.S. Activities* for this session are:

1. Poem Pushers:

The children are asked to read or recite poems using a scary voice and other added scary sounds.

2. Song Squeezers:

Favorite songs are sung in a scary way with a chorus of moaning and groaning added by a separate group.

3. Show Stoppers:

A scary adventure about a person named "Fearless" is created by the children. Fearless can face one scary adventure after another, always coming out the winner of the day.

Evaluation

SELF-PROGRESS CHECK

	Extremely	*Very*	*Reasonably*	*Slightly*	*Not at All*
1. How comfortable was I during the session?					
2. Were the children comfortable during the session?					
3. Were the children willing to share feelings freely?					
4. How well did the children accept the feelings of others?					
5. How accepting was I of the children's responses?					
6. How eager were the children to participate?					
7. How well did the children listen?					
8. Was the environment supportive and safe?					
9. How effective were the questions that I asked?					
10. How interested did the group appear to be?					

Session Fourteen: Freeing Fear

Rationale

"Sometimes I'm afraid of being afraid."

K. Morrison

Goals

To share feelings of fear.
To identify and accept responsibility for feelings of fear.

Materials

Dough ready for shaping and baking (frozen commercial dough in small containers), *Fear Face*; small pieces of paper; jam or butter; brown paper or tin foil; oven; pans; hot pads; napkins; *Reinforcement Activity: Door of Fear.*

Thought Catcher:
"GEORGIE PORGIE'

Georgie Porgie, pudding and pie,
Kissed the girls, and made them cry.
When the boys came out to play,
Georgie Porgie ran away.

Process Activities

A. DISCUSSION STARTERS:

1. Please describe how you think Georgie felt when he was with the girls, and then when the boys came out.
2. Do you feel brave in some situations and then something or someone comes and you feel scared?
3. Have you ever been picked on? Please share your feelings and thoughts.
4. Have you ever picked on others? Please share your feelings and thoughts.
5. How come Georgie ran away? Was he afraid? If so, of what?

B. REINFORCEMENT ACTIVITY:

Individuals write a fear on their *Fear Door* and share it with the group if they wish. Sharing is encouraged, but identification and writing of real fears is to be kept in private.

C. FEARFUL DOUGH ACTIVITY:

Everyone is given a piece of soft dough. After feeling it for a few minutes, the children are asked to make something that reminds them of fear or a fearful object. These fear shapes are then baked. (Shapes can be placed on brown paper or tin foil with the child's name on it.)

D. FEAR FACE (Step one):

While the fear shapes bake, the facilitator passes out small pieces of paper. Individuals are then asked to write what they fear most in the world. (Younger children can hold the face in front of their face and share verbally.) These slips of paper are put in the mouth of the *Fear Face.* (This face can be kept in the room for sharing of other fears throughout the year.)

E. FEAR FEAST:

The fear shapes are shared. What they are and why they were made the way they were is discussed. After the sharing, the shapes are eaten with butter or jam.

F. FEAR FACE (Step two):

The fear feelings are taken out of the face and read. A time of open sharing about these fears follows each shared fear.

Curricular-Related Activities

A. ART:

Make two-faced (two-sided) Georgies that can later be hung in the room. One side has a brave face, the other an afraid face.

B. DRAMA:

Act out the parts of *Georgie Porgie*. Share feelings.

C. GYM (Physical Education):

Two lines are formed at each end of a room. One line is boys and the other, "Georgie Porgies." The Georgie Porgie line walks forward, teasing. Then the facilitator yells: "Run, Georgie, run ! " and the boys chase the "Georgie Porgies" back to their goal. Those persons caught become "boys." The last "Georgie Porgie" becomes the caller for the next game.

D. FORMING (Language Arts):

The children are asked to write a mystery story based on the *Georgie Porgie* caper. Why did Georgie kiss girls? Why did he run? Who was after him? The stories can be shared.

Pretending Time

A minimum of 15-20 minutes should be allocated for this activity.

A. READY-SET-GO:

The children are asked to get into comfortable positions. Then the facilitator says: "Please become quiet. . . Just listen to the music and relax. . . (The music is played for two to three minutes.) Relax...."

B. PRETENDING:

The facilitator says: "Today, I want you to imagine you are a ball of bright light. . . You are happy and full of energy. . . Suddenly, you are hit by a fear ball, and it sticks to you. . . How do you feel? Now, once again, a fear ball comes charging at you, hits you and sticks . . . A few minutes later, another fear ball hits you. . . Look at yourself. . . How do you feel? . . . What do you want to do? . . . Do it. . . Now, how do you feel? . . . How do you look? . . . The fear balls have stopped coming...."

C. STOP-LOOK-LISTEN:

The facilitator says: "All is quiet. . . You begin to relax again. . . Things are okay. . . You relax some more. . . The fear ball falls off. You are safe. . . Enjoy relaxing for a few moments. . . Now, when you are ready, listen to yourself as you look back at the pretending. . . What was learned? . . . Listen to yourself. . . To others. . . ."

D. REFLECTIONS:

The facilitator may ask the following questions:

1. How did you feel as a ball of happy light?
2. What did you think and feel as the first fear ball hit you and stuck?
3. What was it like being covered with fear balls?
4. What did you do?
5. Do you ever feel covered with fear in real life?
6. What can people do about their fears?
7. What is one fear you would like to get rid of? How can you?

Fable:
"THE FIRST CAMEL EVER SEEN"

The first time they ever saw a camel, men were frightened and overwhelmed at its size. As time went on and they saw how gentle it was, they screwed up their courage enough to come close. Then, as they gradually learned that it was not ill-tempered, they came to think so little of the camel that they even put a bridle on it and let the children drive it.

FOLLOW-UP QUESTIONS:

1. Are some things or some people scary at first?
2. Were you scared when you first came to school? Are you still scared in school once in a while?
3. What scares you most?
4. What were you once scared of but aren't anymore?
5. How did you stop being scared of whatever it was?

Supplemental Activities

SENSE STRETCHERS:

Some suggested *Sense Stretchers* that might be used in this session are:

1. Eyes:

The children are asked to draw a scene or item that causes them to feel scared and share this with the others.

2. Ears:

A tape recording of scary sounds can be made by the children. A discussion after listening to the tape can center on what people can do when they hear scary sounds.

3. Nose:

The children close their eyes and imagine what a scary smell might be like. These smells are then shared with the group.

4. Tongue:

The children create an imaginary or real *Fear Feast.* Items can be made and brought in like scary soup (which is dark in color), creepy carrots (which have chocolate sauce poured on them) or horrible hot dogs (which are covered with pretzel sticks).

P. S. (POST SCRIPT) ACTIVITIES:

Some suggested *P.S. Activities* for this session are:

1. Poem Pushers:

The children are asked to pick any poem character and state what they would fear if they were really that person.

2. Song Squeezers:

A favorite melody is chosen and then scary words or sounds and action added to it. The song is then sung by the children.

3. Show Stoppers:

The children individually give themselves a scary name and then stand up to share all the scary adventures this person has experienced. A time limit may have to be imposed on this activity.

Evaluation

PERSONAL NOTES

The purpose of the personal notes is to allow and aid reflection. It is important for the facilitator to look back and recapitulate what has occurred thus far and to write down thoughts, feelings and experiences which have happened during the session.

Frequently, progress is difficult to detect while actively engaged in the session. The personal notes will help promote and provide perceivable progress.

Session Fifteen:
Fear:
Bad Guy—Good Guy Feelings

Rationale

"Knowing when to be afraid helps."

K. Morrison

Goals

To identify the role of fear in life.
To share fear feelings.
To identify and accept responsibility for fearful feelings in self and others.

Materials

Good Guy Hat; Bad Guy Hat; Fear Cards; Reinforcement Activity: Door of Fear; *Suggested Reward* and *Reinforcement Sticker*: I am responsible for my feelings of fear.

Thought Catcher:
"PUSSY CAT, PUSSY CAT"

Pussy cat, pussy cat, where have you been?"
"I've been to London to look at the Queen."
"Pussy cat, pussy cat, what did you there?"
"I frightened a little mouse under a chair."

Process Activities

A. DISCUSSION STARTERS:

1. What part of the Pussy Cat's trip was most important to it? Why?
2. Do you know people who like to scare other people?
3. When someone scares you, how do you feel about that person?
4. Do you like to protect others sometimes?
5. Do you also like for others to protect you at times?

B. BAD GUY-GOOD GUY ACTIVITY:

The facilitator opens a discussion on fear being both a friend (Good Guy) and a foe (Bad Guy). When fear protects us from physical and mental harm it is good. But, when it keeps us from enjoying or seeing life clearly and honestly, it can be bad.

Next, the facilitator brings out the two hats and places them on two stools or chairs in front of the children. A child is then chosen to be a listener and a chooser of one of the hats. The facilitator then verbally describes a situation and the child decides which hat fits that situation. The child then puts on the chosen hat and sits on the stool or chair. Different situations and different children keep the hats and stools in a constant state of change. Later in the activity, the children can make up their own situations.

Situation Examples

John sees a black cat walk in front of him. (Bad Guy).

Tom wonders if he should go swimming alone. (Good Guy)

Ken is playing near railroad tracks and hears a train. (Good Guy)

Larry is afraid of all men with beards. (Bad Guy)

Sally won't try roller skating. (Good Guy)

C. FEAR WHIP:

Everyone sits in a circle. Then one by one they fill in this sentence: "When I am afraid, I ________________. (Repeat 3-4 times).

D. FEAR CARDS:

Cards with various fears are placed in a black or dark box. An individual pulls one out and the card is read aloud. Then the individual and the group decide on different measures the person might use to combat this fear.

Suggested Card Ideas

1. Grade on Test
2. Lightening
3. Monsters
4. Darkness
5. Home Alone
6. Being Late
7. Swimming
8. Away at Camp
9. A Dream
10. Report Card

E. SHARING TIME:

Open discussion about fear.

F. REINFORCEMENT STICKER:

I am responsible for my feelings of fear. The sticker is given out or material to make them is supplied.

G. SUGGESTED REWARD:

Agreed upon rewards for the *Fear Door* are awarded.

Curricular-Related Activities

A. ART:

A paper is divided into two by a dark line. One side has "PUSSYCAT—MEAN FEELING" above it; the other side has "MOUSE—SCARED FEELINGS."

Then the children paint, color or draw in the way those feelings might look.

B. DRAMA:

Act out the parts, even the chair. Check feelings.

C. GYM (Physical Education):

A circle is formed. Someone is the "Pussy Cat" that walks around the circle touching heads and saying: "Purr-purr." But, when Pussy Cat touches a head and says a loud: "Meow-meow," that person becomes the mouse and runs one way, the cat the other way. The first one back can be Pussy Cat for the next round.

D. FORMING (Language Arts):

Children are asked to write a story about *The Scariest Thing in the World*. The story is shared or displayed for others to read.

Pretending Time

A minimum of 15-20 minutes should be allocated for this activity.

A. READY-SET-GO:

The children get into comfortable positions. Then the facilitator says: "Please let yourself become quiet. . . Just relax. . . Sit quietly and listen to the music. . . (The music is played for two to three minutes.)

B. PRETENDING:

The facilitator says: "Today, I want you to take a few moments to think about some things you are afraid of. . . Now, pick one of these things and put it near you. . . Look at it closely. . . What do you see? . . . What do you feel? . . . Now, tell this fear thing exactly what you think of it. . . What does the fear thing do or say? . What do you do or say? . . . Now, take this fear thing and put it somewhere. . . Now, walk away. . . Look back one. . . What is the fear thing doing? . . . What do you feel? . . . Now, continue walking away. . . ."

C. STOP-LOOK-LISTEN:

The facilitator says: "Slowly walk away from this thing you fear. Stop pretending, you no longer have to look back because it is gone . . . You can begin to think. . . Look back over the pretending. . . What did you learn? . . . Listen to what others learned during the pretending. . . ."

D. REFLECTIONS:

The facilitator may ask the following questions:

1. What things were you afraid of?
2. Which thing did you choose to look at?
3. When you looked closely at this thing, what did you see? How did you feel?
4. What did you say to this thing?
5. What did this fearful thing say or do?
6. Where did you put this fearful thing?
7. After you walked away and looked back, what did you see? How did you feel?
8. What can you do about a real fear in your life?

Fable:
"THE BOBTAILED FOX"

A fox had its tail cut off by a trap and was so ashamed that it found life intolerable. The fox decided that it must persuade other foxes to share its condition so that it could conceal its own loss in the common misfortune. Therefore, the fox called them together and urged that a tail was not only an unsightly thing, but that it was an added burden that they were obliged to carry.

One of the foxes interrupted and said, "My dear friend, if this weren't to your advantage, you wouldn't be offering us your advice."

FOLLOW-UP QUESTIONS:

1. How come this fox was so worried about losing its tail?
2. Has something about you ever changed, and then you felt different than others?
3. Is it okay or not okay to be different in some ways than others?
4. Was the fox thinking about itself or its friends when it asked them to cut off their tails?
5. Do you think the other foxes decided to cut off their tails to be like the *Bobtailed Fox*? Would you have?

Supplemental Activities

SENSE STRETCHERS:

1. Eyes:

The children are asked to close their eyes and see something or someone that is scary to them. These scary things can be shared by those who wish. A discussion about what someone can do when they see scary things or people can follow.

2. Ears:

A scary words or sounds contest can be held. The children give their scariest sounds and then a *Boo Button* is given to the winner. Buttons can be made out of any type of material.

3. Nose:

The children are given the opportunity to smell "pretend" smelling salts. Then they share a real or imagined time when they might be so scared that they could faint away in fear.

4. Tongue:

The children can create a store shelf on paper or in the room that contains cans, bottles and other containers of products from the Scary Company.

P. S. (POST SCRIPT) ACTIVITIES:

Some suggested *P.S. Activities* for this session are:

1. Poem Pushers:

A discussion about feelings is acted out by the children taking the roles of Miss Muffet and the spider, Georgie Porgie and the boys and Pussy Cat and the Mouse.

2. Song Squeezers:

A favorite song is chosen. Then, five individuals or groups sing that song expressing one of the following feelings: Happy, Sad, Angry, Unkind and Afraid. The best version wins the honor of choosing the next song.

3. Show Stoppers:

A melodrama is created having characters that demonstrate the feelings of Fear, Unkindness, Sadness, Anger and Happiness. This is best done by having a short outline of the plot and then by assigning characters. The facilitator should let the scene unfold at will. The more over-acted, the better.

Evaluation

1. What I liked *best* about the Fear Feelings Sessions was ____________________
2. What I liked *least* about the Fear Feelings Sessions was ____________________
3. What I wanted to happen in these Fear Feelings Sessions which *never* came about was ____________________
4. During the Fear Feelings Sessions, I wish I would have— ____________________
5. My overall *feelings* about the Fear Feelings Sessions are ____________________

unit six

good feelings

This concluding unit concentrates on positive feelings. as it was important to begin in a positive manner, it is equally important to conclude in a similar manner.

These final experiences emphasize good feelings and serve to integrate the thrust of the book which is, of course, feeling good about me.

The materials needed for the next three sessions are presented here for your preparation.

SESSION SIXTEEN: LIFE'S SPECIAL GIFT IS YOU

Box with mirror inside; drawing paper; paints or crayons or scissors and glue; pencils; paper bag with shape drawn on it; dark shapes with short stories written on them; colorful circles of various sizes for *Reinforcement Activity: The Circle.*

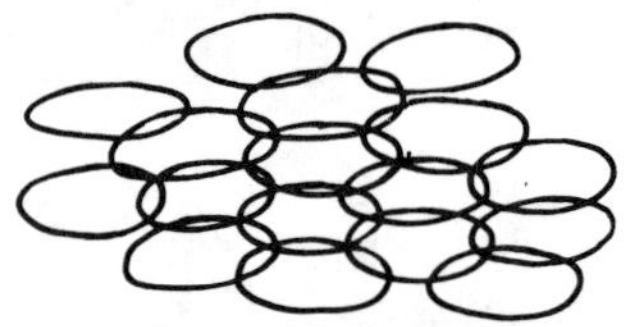

SESSION SEVENTEEN: GOOD FEELINGS GIVEN ARE GOOD FEELINGS RECEIVED

A scale; box of blocks; bowl of popcorn, pretzels, crackers and so forth: circles for *Reinforcement Activity: The Circle.*

In sessions 17 and 18 the children will share one or more experiences of giving or receiving good feelings. After each sharing, a colorful circle is chosen and put up by that child. A beautiful circle design will result.

SESSION EIGHTEEN: FEELING GOOD IS AN ACT OF WILL

Drawing paper; crayons or paints; circles for *Reinforcement Activity: The Circle*; *Suggested Reward; Reinforcement Sticker:* I feel good about me, (or material to make them).

Session Sixteen:
Life's Special Gift is You

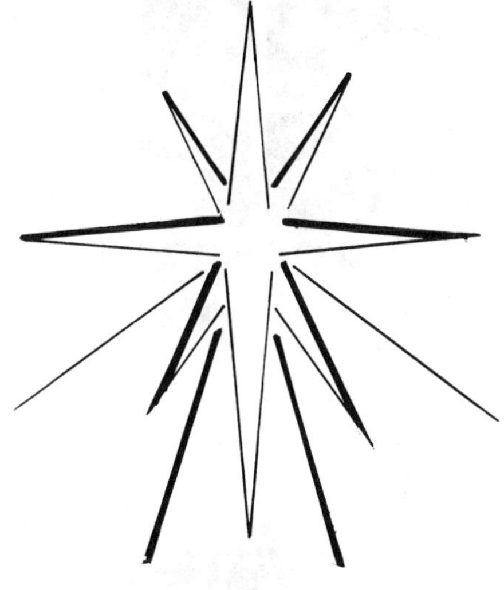

Rationale

"One's self is like a bright shinning star."

K. Morrison

Goals

To identify the specialness of each individual.
To share this specialness with others.
To claim ownership and responsibility of individual talents, abilities and needs.

Materials

Box with mirror inside; drawing paper; paints or crayons or scissors and glue; pencils; paper bag with shape drawn on it; dark shapes with short stories written on them; colorful circles of various sizes for *Reinforcement Activity: The Circle.*

Thought Catcher:
"TWINKLE, TWINKLE, LITTLE STAR"

Twinkle, twinkle, little star,
How I wonder what you are!
Up above the world so high,
Like a diamond in the sky.

When the blazing sun is gone,
When he nothing shines upon;
Then you show your little light,
Twinkle, twinkle, all the night.

Process Activities

A. DISCUSSION STARTERS:

1. Do you ever wish you understood stars, animals or people better?
2. Do things sometimes seem mysterious, far away or strange?
3. Do you think anybody ever wonders what you are really like—really wants to understand and know you better?
4. Do stars really hide in the daylight, or is it just that we can't see them?
5. Do people sometimes hide their feelings, thoughts and talents? Can you think of some reasons why they might do this?

B. THE MAGIC BOX:

The facilitator shows the children a box and explains that it is a *Magic Box* because inside is the face of the most important person in the world. Then the facilitator asks for everyone to promise not to tell who that person is until all children have had a chance to look inside. Then, one by one, the children come forward to see themselves reflected in the mirror.

This is followed by a discussion about why the person they saw is so very important and special. This exercise may be very hard for some children (adults, too), so the individual talents or abilities may need to be identified by others, making sure everyone has something special said about them. (Physical traits are acceptable, but they should not be the major focus.) Everyone should identify one internal quality of value, no matter how small it may seem at the time.

C. THE ME TREE:

Children are asked to make and share a *Me Tree*. This tree can be drawn, painted or made out of construction paper. The tree has three main parts—successes in life, dreams and hopes, and things you or other people like in you.

These trees are shared and then put up as part of room decorations. (Younger children may need help writing in words; they can draw pictures or cut out pictures from magazines.)

D. THE YOU HIDE:

A bag with a U on it (having various dark shapes with short stories written on them inside) is shown to the children. The facilitator explains that we all have things we don't like about ourselves. These things will always be part of our lives, but many times they can become too important and can hold people back from doing or being who they want to be. Many times, if these hidden things are brought out into the light, they look less scary and important and can even disappear or be changed. Hiding things from others usually doesn't seem to help.

The children then are given turns to reach inside, take one shape out of the bag, read the little story and talk about what that pretend person could do to stop hiding that specific feeling.

Examples of stories:

1. Tommy got a low grade in spelling. He crumpled it up and hid it in the back of his desk.
2. Susan saw Mary with a new bike. She hoped Mary would fall off and hurt herself and the bike. Susan felt funny the next time she saw Mary.
3. Jim saw a sad movie on television. He felt like crying but tried to hide it so his brother wouldn't see tears.

E. SHARING TIME:

Everyone is asked to share one or two things they really like about themselves and want to keep. If this is too hard for some, suggestions from the group are acceptable. If the children can stand up when they speak, it will add to the specialness and importance of that person.

F. CLOSING QUESTIONS:

The facilitator asks:

1. Is it okay to like yourself?
2. Is it okay to like who you are, which includes all your hopes, dreams, successes and failures?

G. REINFORCEMENT ACTIVITY:

The facilitator introduces the circle and explains the rules of the activity and the reward.

Curricular-Related Activities

A. ART:

The children make individual stars with their names on them and hang them over their desks. The more glitter, tin foil and so forth, the better.

B. DRAMA:

Choose several children to be stars. They are to sit down together and talk over their plans for the night, sharing their fears and hopes for the evening. This can be repeated several times. A sun, moon, cloud and storm can be added to the cast of characters.

C. GYM (Physical Education):

A circle is formed. One child is chosen to be the *Star* and stand in the center of the circle. Holding hands, the circle moves to the right while saying: "Twinkle, twinkle, little star, How I wonder what you are. Up above the world so high, Like a diamond in the sky." At the word "sky," the children drop hands and move three steps in any direction. The *Star* can then take ten steps. As soon as another child is touched, that person becomes the *Star.*

D. FORMING (Language Arts):

The children may write a story about a star who would not shine, called *Dim Light.* The story can include reasons why the star would not shine and a possible solution or happy ending. Another activity might be a list of words that have star quality—examples might be: shiny, bright, glows and so forth.

Pretending Time

A minimum of 15-20 minutes should be allocated for this activity.

A. READY-SET-GO:

The children get into comfortable positions. The facilitator says: "Please sit quietly. . . Enjoy the quiet. . . A soft, gentle, warm breeze is now coming into the room. . . It comes over to you. . . It is warm and gentle. . . It begins to touch you. . . It is warm, safe, gentle. . . You are surrounded by this warm, gentle safe breeze... Enjoy this feeling for a few moments...."

B. PRETENDING:

The facilitator says: "Today, you can become a beautiful shiny star, all sparkling and glowing. . . How does it feel to be such a star? . . . It is a clear night and you are shining brightly. . . Take a few moments now to talk with the other stars around you. . . Now, the moon is moving closer to you. . . As this star, how do you feel about the moon? . . . Talk to the moon. . . Suddenly, you feel a cold wind covering you, and you notice dark clouds coming toward you . . . How do you feel about the coming storm? . . .

You are now completely surrounded by cold wind and dark clouds. . . What can you say to yourself to feel better? . . . What can you do? . . . Now the storm has passed and you are once again free to shine and glow. . . How does this feel? . . . Spend a few moments being that very special star. . . And, now, it is time to slowly stop. . . ."

C. STOP-LOOK-LISTEN:

The facilitator says: "They sky is quiet. . . Stop pretending. . . Slowly, the morning sun begins to lighten the sky. . . Take time now to think over the pretending. . . What did you learn? . . . Can you share it with others? . . . Listen. . . Let others share with you."

D. REFLECTIONS:

The facilitator may ask the following questions:

1. How did you feel being the bright shiny star?
2. What did you do as this star?
3. What did you say to the moon?
4. What were your thoughts and feelings as the cold wind covered you?
5. As a star, what did the dark clouds mean to you?
6. How did you feel about the coming storm?
7. When you were surrounded by the storm clouds, what did you say to feel better?
8. What did you think or feel when the storm went away?
9. In real life, have you ever felt real good and then someone or something changed that feeling? When?
10. When unhappy things happen to you, what can you do to feel better?

Fable:
"THE HAWKS AND THE SWANS"

Nature originally gave the hawks as fine a voice as she did the swans. But, when the hawks heard the horses' whinny, they fell in love with the sound and, in trying to imitate it, lost what they had plus what they were trying to learn: They didn't learn to whinny and they forgot how to sing.

FOLLOW-UP QUESTIONS:

1. Do you think the hawks were trying to be something they weren't?
2. Have you ever admired a quality of another person and tried to copy it? If so, what happened?
3. Do you know some people who try to copy other people?
4. How do you think the hawks felt when they forgot how to sing?
5. Have you ever lost something you had because you weren't satisfied with it?

Supplemental Activities

SENSE STRETCHERS:

Some suggested *Sense Stretchers* that might be used in this session are:

1. Eyes:

The children are asked to share the things and people in their life they would call "good."

2. Ears:

The children are asked to share sounds and words that sound good to their ears.

3. Nose:

The children are asked to share good smells.

4. Tongue:

The children are asked to share good tastes.

P. S. (POST SCRIPT) ACTIVITIES:

1. Poem Pushers:

The children choose a good character in any poem and state why they think that person is good.

2. Song Squeezers:

Favorite songs are sung just to have a good time together. In addition, a pretend fire around which to sing (or a hike to a special spot) can be a good culminating activity for all the songs sung in this program.

3. Show Stoppers:

A soap box is provided for one minute political speeches on *Our Need for Goodness in This World.* A Mock Election for the best candidate to bring such goodness to the world can then be held.

Evaluation

SELF-EVALUATION PROGRESS CHECK

	Extremely	*Very*	*Reasonably*	*Slightly*	*Not at All*
1. How comfortable was I during the session?					
2. Were the children comfortable during the session?					
3. Were the children willing to share feelings freely?					
4. How well did the children accept the feelings of others?					
5. How accepting was I of the children's responses?					
6. How eager were the children to participate?					
7. How well did the children listen?					
8. Was the environment supportive and safe?					
9. How effective were the questions that I asked?					
10. How interested did the group appear to be?					

Session Seventeen: Good Feelings Given are Good Feelings Received

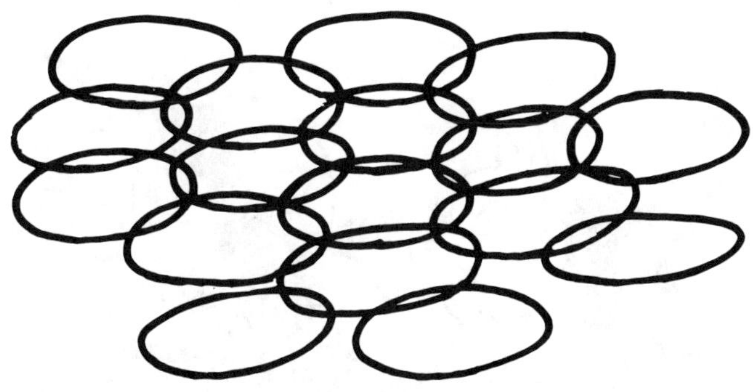

Rationale

"I feel good when others feel good too."

K. Morrison

Goals

To identify and claim good feelings and caring for others.
To accept the responsibility and right to like and care for others.
To share good feelings with others.
To explore new ways of discovering, developing and demonstrating good feelings.

Materials

A scale; box of blocks; bowl of popcorn, pretzels, crackers and so forth; circles for *Reinforcement Activity: The Circle.*

Thought Catcher:
"I LOVE LITTLE PUSSY"

**I love little pussy, her coat is so warm,
And if I don't hurt her, she'll do me no harm.
So I'll not pull her tail, nor drive her away,
But, pussy and I very gently will play.
I'll sit by the fire, and give her some food,
And pussy will love me because I am good.**

Process Activities

A. DISCUSSION STARTERS:

1. Would you like the person in the poem to be your friend? Why or why not?
2. Have you ever been mistreated or hurt by someone bigger than you?
3. Have you ever felt like hurting someone or something? Please explain.
4. Do you think people like you only when you are good? What does "good" mean to you?
5. Can you share a time when someone took extra good care of you? How did you feel?
6. Can you share a time when you took extra good care of someone? How did you feel?

B. REINFORCEMENT ACTIVITY:

The facilitator and the children share experiences in which they have given or received good feelings. As the children share experiences, circles are added to the larger circle design.

C. GOOD FEELINGS SCALE

A scale (Preferrably a double scale) and a box are used for this activity. As individuals name people they feel good about, a block is put on the "out" side of the feeling good scale. As the individuals mention people who feel good about them, a block is placed on the "in" side of the feeling good scale. If only a one-sided scale is available, then the "in" and "out" are weighed separately. At the end of this activity there should be a good indication of the positive feelings in each person's life. A time of sharing and reacting is recommended as a follow-up activity.

D. THE WAITING GAME:

A circle is formed by the children facing outward. One child is asked to sit in the center of the circle. The children then begin to whisper softly to each other, ignoring the child in the center.

After about two or three minutes, the facilitator (or some appointed child) will turn around and say something nice to the child in the center. The rest of the circle follows this pattern.

This activity is done four or five times and then the experience is shared. The facilitator focuses on how others felt being left out, leaving others out, being included and including others.

E. THE CIRCLE (Sharing Time):

The children sit in a circle and share a good feelings feast. A bowl of crackers, popcorn or pretzels is passed from one to the other. Each time food is taken, the individual shares why it is important for them to feel good about themselves.

F. QUESTION TIME:

The facilitator asks the following questions:

1. Is it okay to express or show your good feelings for someone first? Or, should you wait?
2. Are good feelings ever scary? When? Why?
3. Are good feelings ever bad?
4. Can you work at feeling good about someone?
5. Do good feelings usually grow as you know someone better?
6. When you share good feelings, what happens to you? To the other person?

Curricular-Related Activities

A. ART:

From cotton (body), paper (ears, nose, mouth) and broomstraw (whiskers), the children can make a pussy cat of their own. This cat can be named and placed on the desk or taken home to be loved, held and petted. Special ribbon or bows can be added, or even a box house or box bed can be made.

B. DRAMA:

Soliloquy—The children and the facilitator come forward to sit on a stool or chair and talk as if they were the "Pussy Cat" in the poem. Each person can talk about how it feels being a cared-for cat and, perhaps, about some other adventures.

C. GYM (Physical Education):

This activity can be based on physical fitness requirements of a school or those chosen by the facilitator. A stuffed cat is placed at the end of a series of physical feats. Some requirements might be a somersault, walking a line, jumping across a space, hopping or jumping rope. The activity can be made into an adventure of saving the pussy cat by making the physical feats part of a pretend adventure.

Examples of this might be jumping a stream, walking a high and narrow cliff, rolling down a hill, hopping rocks across a fast-moving river, climbing a hill (ladder) and jumping jungle ropes. It can be as exciting as the facilitator chooses to make it.

D. FORMING (Language Arts):

A letter is written to someone special. This letter is personal. What is done with it is up to the individual child. Writing personal feelings down is an important part of identifying and claiming feelings.

A second and safer letter which can be shared could be a letter to or from the Pussy Cat.

Pretending Time

A minimum of 15-20 minutes should be allocated for this activity.

A. READY-SET-GO:

The children get into comfortable positions. Then the facilitator says: "Please close your eyes... Enjoy the quiet... A soft, warm, gentle color is entering the room... Look at it... It slowly and gently comes toward you... It gently surrounds you... It is a warm, gentle color... You are completely surrounded by this friendly color... Just enjoy it for a few more moments...."

B. PRETENDING:

The facilitator says: "The gentle color slowly fades away... But, you remain relaxed... Today, I want you to become a good feeling... How do you look as a good feeling? ... How do you feel? Now, I want you to find some place where you are needed as a good feeling; some place where you can be safe and grow and feel welcome... Please take a few moments now to find that place... Now that you have found that place, look around... What do you see? ... How do you feel? ... Now, I want you to start growing... What ever you need to grow you can find nearby, use it... You are bigger and stronger now... Does this make the place you are in feel or look different? ... Look around, has anything changed? ... The time has now come to leave this place... How do you feel about leaving? ... Before you leave, you may leave a gift— anything you want... Please choose a gift... Leave this gift someplace...."

C. STOP-LOOK-LISTEN:

The facilitator says: "Now, stop pretending. . . You must leave. . . Say 'good bye' . . . You have done a good job. . . Take time to think. . . Take time to learn about what you were pretending. . . Take time to listen to others. . . What was learned?"

D. REFLECTIONS:

The facilitator may ask the following questions:

1. How did you look as a good feeling?
2. How did you feel?
3. What place did you find to live and grow?
4. What did the place look like?
5. What did you need to grow?
6. What did the place look like after you grew?
7. How did you feel about leaving?
8. What gift did you leave?
9. What good feelings have you received from someone in real life?
10. Share a good feeling you have given someone else.

Fable:
"THE FOAL

A man was riding a mare (a mother horse) and her baby (a foal) was following behind them, on a trip. The foal followed right along behind its mother, but its strength soon gave out. Then the foal said to its mother's rider, "See how very small I am and unfit to travel. But, consider that if you leave me here, I shall die without delay. If, on the other hand, you carry me from here, take me home and have me reared, there will come a time when I grow up and let you ride me."

FOLLOW-UP QUESTIONS:

1. Do you feel that sometimes you have to let your point of view be known or others do not seem to notice you?
2. Do you think the rider has good feelings about the foal?
3. Do you think animal parents have feelings about their babies the same as do human parents?
4. If you were the man, would you carry the foal?
5. Do you sometimes give or share good feelings to receive good feelings from others?

Supplemental Activities

SENSE STRETCHERS:

1. Eyes:

The children are asked to close their eyes and imagine something good with their "mind's eye." This activity may then be shared with the group.

2. Ears:

The children are given a small card on which they can write good words and then these cards are read aloud. (Save these cards for use in session eighteen.)

3. Nose:

The children are asked to bring an object that smells good to them and this object is passed around for all to experience.

4. Tongue:

The children are blindfolded and various items are given to them to taste and decide if it tastes good. Such items could be a piece of pickle, bread, rasins, peanuts, lettuce and so forth. After each item, blindfolds are removed and a vote is taken. Then the item is disclosed.

P. S. (POST SCRIPT) ACTIVITIES:

Some suggested *P.S. Activities* for this session are:

1. Poem Pushers:

Poems are read or recited by children using any of the feelings of Happiness, Anger, Sadness, Unkindness, Fear and Goodness. This can be a guessing game for the group to play. The children attempt to guess which of the feelings is being presented.

2. Song Squeezers:

Songs are sung to demonstrate any of the six feeling areas.

3. Show Stoppers:

The children may choose to develop and act out any of the six feelings in play form. The short play may be given for the rest of the group.

Evaluation

PERSONAL NOTES

The purpose of the personal notes is to allow and aid reflection. It is important for the facilitator to look back and recapitulate what has occurred thus far and to write down thoughts, feelings and experiences which have happened during the session.

Frequently, progress is difficult to detect while actively engaged in the session. The personal notes will help promote and provide perceivable progress.

____

____

____

____

____

____

____

____

Session Eighteen: Feeling Good is a Personal Choice

Rationale

"Choosing to have good feelings is the first step in the development of a positive self-image."

K. Morrison

Goals

To identify areas where we limit good feelings.
To risk, to reach out, to accept failures, faults and differences in self and others and still be able to have good feelings.

Materials

Drawing paper; crayons or paints; circles for *Reinforcement Activity: The Circle; Suggested Reward; Reinforcement Sticker;* I feel good about me (or material to make them).

Thought Catcher:
"MOLLY, MY SISTER AND I"

Molly, my sister, and I fell out,
And what do you think it was all about?
She loved coffee and I loved tea,
And that was the reason we couldn't agree.

Process Activities

A. DISCUSSION STARTERS:

1. Was Molly or her sister in the right in this poem?
2. Do you know people who fight over seemingly small things?
3. What things are worth losing a friend for?
4. Name one person you feel good about, and one thing you may not agree with that that person does or says. How does this affect your relationship?
5. Is it easier to have good feelings about people who are like or who are different from ourselves?
6. Is being different wrong?

B. REINFORCEMENT ACTIVITY:

The facilitator and the children share experiences of loving and add circles to *The Circle.*

C. THE UNLOVEABLES:

Every child draws something (monster, object) that they deem unloveable. When everyone is finished, the *Unloveables* are introduced and explained why they are unloveable. Then the drawings are exchanged and the *Unloveables* are introduced again with a different child giving an explanation why the *Unloveable* is the way it is and how it feels being an *Unloveable.* The *Unloveables* are then returned to the original owners.

D. THE LOVEABLE/UNLOVEABLE COMMERCIAL:

Small groups or individuals create short commercials trying to see the *Unloveables* as being loveable. These high-powered commercials are then presented to the group.

E. SHARING TIME:

The facilitator begins a discussion about how children felt first about their *Unloveable* and how they feel about it now. Then they are asked to share experiences in which they thought they wouldn't like a person, thing or food, but found out differently.

F. QUESTION TIME:

The facilitator asks the following questions of the children:

1. Do we have to have good feelings about everyone?
2. Do we sometimes limit our good feelings by being afraid of something new or different?
3. Do we sometimes think we can't have good feelings because we seem different from other people?
4. Can having good feelings be the best experience in life?

G: REINFORCEMENT STICKER:

I feel good about me the good feelings stickers are handed or materials to make the stickers are provided.

H. SUGGESTED REWARD:

At this point, a discussion concerning internal and external rewards could take place. It is probably appropriate at this time in the program to help children further understand the satisfaction found in internal rewards.

Curricular-Related Activities

A. ART:

Individuals or small groups of children create a *Good Feelings Poster* to be displayed somewhere outside their area. Posters may encourage sharing and caring or discourage acts of dis-concern or harm.

B. DRAMA: The children can act out the scene of the two sisters fighting over tea and coffee. This can be followed by the children creating their own scenes of two people arguing over differences in likes and dislikes.

C. GYM (Physical Education):

Two even-numbered lines are formed at both ends of a large room. One line is called the "Tea Tasters" and the other is called the "Coffee Klache." The lines count off from opposite ends, then the facilitator calls off a number and both children with that number run to the center of the room.

The facilitator then calls out "Tea" or "Coffee" and the child from that team tries to run home before being tagged by the child from the opposite team. The child, if tagged, must return to the opposite team. The team with the most people wins.

D. FORMING (Language Arts):

The children are asked to write dialogue between a cup of tea and a cup of coffee on Molly's table. The facilitator can teach the correct punctuation and so forth for writing dialogue, but the main focus remains on the ideas and thoughts shared.

Pretending Time

A minimum of 15-20 minutes should be allocated for this activity.

A. READY-SET-GO:

The children are asked to get into comfortable positions. Then the facilitator says: "Please relax. . . Enjoy the quiet. . . Now, I want you to imagine that a soft, quiet, gentle sound is entering the room. . . Listen to the sound. . . It is quiet and gentle. . . The sound is coming closer to you. . . Look at it. . . Hear it. . . Feel it... The sound now gently and slowly surrounds you . . . Enjoy this feeling. . . This time is just for you. . . You are special. . . Relax in the warm, friendly sound. . . Now, let the sound slowly move away from you. . . The sound is now leaving the room, but you know it will come back whenever you ask it to, so say 'goodbye.'

B. PRETENDING:

The facilitator says: Today, I want you to become a small speck of dirt. . . You are feeling lonely, hot and dry. . . Suddenly, you hear footsteps and then, all at once, you are kicked at and almost stepped on. . . How does it make you feel? . . . You continue to lie there and the hot sun beats down on you. . . Once again, you hear footsteps coming toward you. . . What do you think about? . . . Then, without a warning, you are scooped up with a lot of other pieces of dirt and put in a beautiful, red flower pot. . . What thoughts run through your head when this happens? . . . Now, warm water runs over you. . . And you begin to feel cozy. . . Then you notice a little dry seed right next to you. . . What do you say to the seed? . . . What does the seed say to you? . . . Days and weeks pass. . . The seed grows. . . You help the seed. . . How do you feel about the seed now? . . . How does the seed feel about you? . . . How do you feel about yourself? . . . Now, it is time to stop being that speck of dirt. . . ."

C. STOP-LOOK-LISTEN:

The facilitator says: "Everything seems right now. . . Stop pretending. . . You have found a friend. . . So, just relax. . . Now the time has come to stop being that speck of dirt. . . Begin to think about what you learned while you were pretending. . . What do you think others learned? . . . Listen!

D. REFLECTIONS:

The facilitator may ask the following questions:

1. How did it feel being a speck of dirt that was kicked around?
2. What did you think and feel as you were scooped up and put in a pot?
3. How did the water feel?
4. Tell us what feelings or thoughts you had about the seed.
5. What did you think or feel as the seed began growing?
6. How did the seed feel about you?
7. Did you like being in this pot?
8. In real life, has anyone made you feel small and unimportant? Please explain!
9. When do you feel most at home?
10. Who helps you feel good about life and yourself the most?
11. When you help out someone, how do you feel inside?
12. Is liking yourself an okay thing? Explain why or why not.

Fable:

"THE CUCKOO AND THE BIRDS"

Aesop says that when the cuckoo asked the little birds why they shunned him, they said they were afraid he would turn out to be a hawk;

FOLLOW-UP QUESTIONS:

1. Are there times when you are afraid of something and later find that it is really nothing of which to be afraid?
2. Do you sometimes find that being afraid stops you from getting hurt?
3. Do you ever want people to be afraid of you?
4. Do you ever have good feelings about something of which you are afraid?
5. How do you know when to be afraid and when not to be?

Supplemental Activities

Some suggested *Sense Stretchers* that might be used with this session are:

1. Eyes:

The children are asked to create individually or as a group a picture of what goodness might look like.

2. Ears:

A tape is made of good words. (The words on the cards from session seventeen can be used.) The angry tape is played, followed by the scary tape and then the good tape. Reactions to all the tapes may then be shared.

3. Nose:

The children decide on a food smell that the majority find good. The item is then made or furnished so everyone can enjoy the smell. . .

4. Tongue:

. . . and then this food item is eaten. Examples might be pizza, donuts, cookies, bubble gum, pie, cake, root beer and so forth.

P. S. (POST SCRIPT) ACTIVITIES:

Some suggested *P.S. Activities* for this session are:

1. Poem Pushers:

The poems that have been used in this program are practiced and then shared with another group. The feelings that might have been experienced by characters in each poem can also be shared.

2. Song Squeezers:

Songs that demonstrate the variety of feelings in this program can be practiced and then shared with others.

3. Show Stoppers:

The favorite *Show Stopper* ever presented is given a chance to be re-run. Any new ones can also be shared at this time.

Evaluation

1. What I liked *best* about the Good Feelings Sessions was ______________________________________
2. What I liked *least* about the Good Feelings Sessions was____________________________________
3. What I wanted to happen in these Good Feelings Sessions which *never* came about was____
4. During the Good Feelings Sessions, I wish I would have____________________________________
5. My overall *feelings* about the Good Feelings Sessions are____________________________________

Culminating Activity: Feeling Fair

The *Feeling Fair* is like any other fair where there are a variety of exciting attractions. The *Feeling Fair* also has many areas of interest—next to each attraction is an abbreviation which describes the activity: SS—Side Shows; J—Joker; A—Arcade. Posters advertising the event will add to the excitement and interest.

The idea behind the *Feeling Fair* is to provide a culminating experience for the eighteen sessions which emphasizes positive feelings.

The *Feeling Fair* can be prepared by the children, the parents, or any group of interested individuals under the supervision of the facilitator. Some suggestions for the *Feeling Fair* are given below, but the children will want to add many more creative ideas than are provided.

FEELING FAIR ATTRACTIONS

Suggestions

SS 1. Clown Act:

One or more of the children can dress up and do a prepared series of jokes and/or tricks.

J 2. Joker:

This act can be a stand-up comic who tells a series of jokes and/or someone who has little jokes pasted on clothes and walks around letting people read the jokes, or hands out joke cards, or tells jokes.

A 3. The Haw-Haw House:

An area is set up where funny pictures cover the walls and a tape recording of laughter is constantly played. Chairs or pillows can be provided for those who desire to stay longer.

SS 4. The Queen of Hearts—The King of Hearts:

A child with a large red heart on front and back hands out a candy heart with a message written on it. Different children can be King and Queen.

A 5. Bean Bag Toss:

For this activity you will need a board with a large, happy face and an opening where the mouth is. The children toss bean bags into the open mouth. Prizes are awarded.

J 6. Silly Suckers Seller:

You will need commercially or home-made suckers with happy faces on them. A child in funny clothes is allowed to pass out suckers to others for positive feelings.

A 7. Knock a Feeling Over Game:

For this activity you will need a large soft ball and plastic bowling pins or tall, thin plastic bottles. Label the pins with unkind feelings, sad feelings and so forth. Try to knock the pins down with the ball. Award prizes.

A 8. Fishing for Good Feelings:

For this activity you will need paper fish with good feelings written on them and a paper clip on each. You will also need a stick, string and a magnet to be used as the fishing pole. The good feeling is the prize.

SS 9. I Feel Good About Me Booth:

Children come to the booth and say: "I feel good about me." Each person who says this receives a button as a prize.

Conclusion

These experiences have been developed in such a manner so they help children explore, experience and carefully examine feelings that influence self-image. The purpose of these sessions has been to aid children in the development of positive self-images so they may not only become better students, but also live life more positively and fully.